Y0-BVR-030

LEADERS IN EDUCATION

Their Views on
Controversial Issues

LEADERS IN EDUCATION

Their Views on Controversial Issues

Edited by

Glenda F. Roberson

University of Texas at Tyler

Mary A. Johnson

University of Texas at Tyler

UNIVERSITY
PRESS OF
AMERICA

Lanham • New York • London

Library of Congress Cataloging-in-Publication Data

Leaders in education—their views on controversial issues / Glenda F.
Roberson, Mary A. Johnson, editors.
p. cm
Bibliography: p.
Includes index.
1. Education—United States. 2. Early childhood education—United
States. 3. Educators—United States—Biography. I. Roberson,
Glenda F. II. Johnson, Mary A. (Mary Alice), 1936– .
LB7.L38   1988
370'.973—dc 19   88–19918 CIP
ISBN 0–8191–7122–0 (alk. paper)
ISBN 0–8191–7123–9 (pbk. : alk. paper)

CONTENTS

Preface

Introduction
Valora Washington

ARTICLES

PREFACE

In discussing the needs and concerns of children, future and current teachers frequently ask: "Who are the people in education who speak to the issues? Who addresses such topics as the need for play, children's rights, the effects of technology and media upon children, curriculum development, teaching in a multicultural classroom, mainstreaming, changing family patterns, and historical trends in education? Who are the leaders teachers need to look to for guidance?"

There is a strong desire among both undergraduate and graduate education students to know more about current issues in education and the leaders in education who address them. We better understand the present and can predict the future by looking at the past. In our own work with students, we have felt the need for a text that would serve to identify major leaders in education, to introduce topics of concern, and to offer students a bibliography of each leader's published work. We could find no text that met this criteria; therefore, we began to look at the possibility of editing a book consisting of a collection of articles by invited authors who are known as authorities in the field of education.

Selected leaders in education whose writings regularly appear in refereed journals were invited to contribute to this text. We were gratified and overwhelmed with the positive response and willingness to participate by so many of those invited.

Each leader was asked to address the following topics: their educational background, their mentors, their contribution to the field of education, historical changes in education they have felt significant, current concerns in education, and their perceptions on future trends in education. In addition, each was asked to submit a recent photograph, a short biographical sketch, and a bibliography of selected published works with his/her article.

This text presents a significant and timely body of material authored by those most qualified to identify and address significant issues. It well serve as a major source of information for any person interested in the education of children. By including a profile for each contributor, readers can assess the ideas presented in the light of each author's background.

It is our fervent hope that this text will provide both interesting and useful information reflective of this time in our history. Perhaps in future years, it may be viewed as a classic.

Glenda F. Roberson
The University of Texas at Tyler

Mary A. Johnson
The University of Texas at Tyler

INTRODUCTION

Generations of American presidents, both Democratic and Republican, have pronounced the importance of children and the family in a strong government. Nevertheless, in contrast to promises for a "national commitment" to child development in the early years and pledges to "honor and support and strengthen" the American family, there is little in American social policy, aside from the public schools, which commits the resources of the United States to fulfill these goals for children and families. Indeed, care for children and family support has generally been considered a private matter except in a national emergency, an economic disaster, or a health crisis (Washington, 1985).

The contrast between political/educational rhetoric and actual policy poses a dilemma which affects the well-being of all children. This contrast is important to recognize because it often lies at the core of many controversial issues in education and child development: Should we routinely provide for the care of young children using public resources? Should special assistance be targeted to particular groups, such as the poor or the handicapped? Should services be preventive or rehabilitative? How can the quest for educational excellence be reconciled with issues of equity? What is the role of the learners? Answers to these questions are often complex and relate to issues of appropriate instruction, the role of technology, the professionalism of teaching, the needs of children, and educational reform.

A central focus of these controversies is the need to prepare children -- and ourselves as educators -- to be prepared for unforseeable possibilities and to adapt to rapid change. From this perspective, educators have the challenge of preparing children today for tomorrow's world. Inherent in this challenge is the broader question: What kind of people do we want in the 21st century?

In this volume, leaders in education express their views on these and other challenges facing education in the 1990's. Four themes emerge from their views. First, there is a need for educators to appreciate the importance of social change in shaping outcomes for children. Second, educators must respond to calls for accountability related to student skill development while we continue to help children develop important human values. Third, we must celebrate educational success and continue to learn from our mistakes. And, fourth, an important goal of educational reform must be to examine critically issues related to teacher professionalism, qualifications, and compensation. Each of these themes is discussed below.

* THERE IS A NEED FOR EDUCATORS TO APPRECIATE THE IMPORTANCE OF SOCIAL CHANGE IN SHAPING OUTCOMES FOR CHILDREN.

Educators have too often proceeded as if the development of children occurs in a stable or invariant culture. This assumption is refuted by longitudinal studies and an increased appreciation of the significance of the cultural, historical, social and economic context surrounding education. Therefore, it is not only useful to consider the larger ecological context of education, but also to bear in mind that the ecological context undergoes change as well. Children learn in a changing society, and they themselves later become active contributors to social change. Thus, changes in the macroecological context of education need to be considered in charting and accounting for the when, how, and why of education and in preparing children for later life (Baltes and Brim, 1982). The recognition that "normal" children and families are not insulated from social forces is an important first step in addressing controversial issues in education.

In the midst of growing complexities and educational dilemmas, public policy wil clearly affect education in the coming years as legislators consider reform alternatives and attempt to balance educational inequities. Yet the perceived benefits of broad public attention to education must not obscure a host of specific instructional concerns. In this volume, educational leaders talk about the "basic needs of young children," "caring and kindness," "play," and John Dewey as if to remind us of important human values which must form the core of our response to educational reform and technology in the context of social change.

* EDUCATORS MUST RESPOND TO CALLS FOR ACCOUNTABILITY RELATED TO STUDENT SKILL DEVELOPMENT WHILE WE CONTINUE TO HELP CHILDREN DEVELOP IMPORTANT HUMAN VALUES.

Unlike many legislators and taxpayers, educators have the specific training and experience to offer a professional and long-term perspective to public policy related to children. Educators are particularly prepared to respond to current crises or fads in the ecological context of childhood. It is important to remember that conflicting theories and concepts about education have arisen through time that are accepted and then rejected, reconsidered and reformulated as educators and parents search for the optimum techniques (see Short, this volume).

Today, both legislators and taxpayers are applying increased pressure on schools for a "back-to-basics" curriculum. Partly fueled by reports on the crisis of our educational system, there is a new emphasis on drill, recitation, homework, discipline, testing, traditional grading systems, and the elimination of social promotion (Morrison, 1984). There is honest debate about whether formal instruction is more efficient, more economical, more necessary or more cognitively stimulating than other models of instruction. Advocates of a "whole child" approach are concerned that the back-to-basics movement will make learning an unpleasant, dull, monotonous and rote task. There is also concern that basic skills will become THE curriculum with little emphasis on the social sciences, art, and music.

These calls for accountability challenge teachers to use their knowledge of human development to create an appropriate balance between intellectual, social-emotional and physical growth. A further dilemma is how educators can use the students' own interests and abilities to promote a love of learning and to preserve their emerging self-confidence while addressing the back-to-basics concerns of the taxpayer. Further, educators must remember that we are educating students for the future, not for the rose-colored past (see Shanker, this volume).

The introduction of technologies, such as computers, in the curriculum has served to intensify these controversies. With these technologies emerge new debates: inequitable access to computers based on race, social class and gender is a sensitive new issue. Further, some educators fear that the technology lends itself best to instructional programming based on behavioristic theory.

The importance of helping children to develop important human values in the context of rapid social or technological change is emphasized by various educational leaders throughout this volume. Constance Kamii argues that educators ought to play a part in raising generations who are morally and intellectually autonomous. Ralph Tyler writes that "...education's greatest allies are parents and other people in the community who care about children. Its greatest enemies are cultures and individuals who seek material rewards ahead of human welfare and persons who are indifferent to the human condition." Brian Sutton-Smith's "greatest fear is that in striving for achievement and intellectual excellence we will engender an obedience culture, with little oportunity for individual initiative and originality..."

* WE MUST CELEBRATE EDUCATIONAL SUCCESS AND CONTINUE TO LEARN FROM OUR MISTAKES.

Maintaining a collective memory or a balance between short-and long-term views of education is one service that professional educators can offer to the broader society. Indeed, many of the controversial issues in education are controversial because of the success of the American educational model: commitment to universal, free public education for all children. Educational leaders in this volume reflect on the progress toward school desegregation and the benefits of early intervention -- both successful experiments of the past twenty years (see Washington and Oyemade, 1987). In the midst of intense debate about education, and focus on its many imperfections, it is important to recognize and to celebrate the fact that both educators and society continue to struggle with, rather than simply abandon, these issues.

For example, moving from stark disparities in school enrollment rates 100 years ago, blacks and whites now have virtually identical rates of enrollment. Over the past 15 years, largely due to the success of federal programs such as Head Start and Chapter 1, reading and math achievement scores for blacks have improved dramatically relative to the scores of white students.

The "failures" of our educational system are well-documented and widely discussed. Attention to successes which should be celebrated in no way explains or justifies racial inequities, instructional shortcomings, or institutional reticence. By acknowledging success, however, we gain the perspective and courage needed to risk further experimentation, to learn from our mistakes, and to continue to move forward toward our goals.

* AN IMPORTANT GOAL OF EDUCATIONAL REFORM MUST BE TO EXAMINE CRITICALLY ISSUES RELATED TO TEACHER PROFESSIONALISM, QUALIFICATIONS, AND COMPENSATION.

There has been growing public controversy about the professional status of teachers and teaching; issues related to teacher or program quality, the training and qualification of teachers, program certification, working conditions, and child-staff ratios are capturing the public attention. Between 1983 and 1985, at least 30 national reports and 250 state reports on the status of teaching have been issued, many of which blame the decline in the quality of schooling on the quality of American educators or colleges of education. Further, Joyce and Clift (1984) observe that the field of teacher education "is not just surrounded by critics, it is inhabited by them" (p. 5).

There may be a tremendous gap between what is known and what is practiced in education, partly because education concepts, theories, research and methods have been developed independently of educational practice. One contributor to this volume illustrates this gap through her one-year experience as a classroom teacher following many years of university experience.

Reform in education must be clearly related to measures of effectiveness. Despite the numerous problems involved in doing definitive research on school effects and effective schools, researchers have identified correlates of school effectiveness related to school ideology, organizational structure and instructional practices (e.g. Brookover, 1985; Wadsworth, this volume).

Many controversial measures have been introduced as means to address issues of professional quality and compensation. Unfortunately, some of the solutions, specifically entrance and exit examinations for prospective teachers, effectively perpetuate the scarcity of minority teachers at a time when the proportion of minority students is increasing (see Washington and LaPoint, 1988).

In conclusion, the reader of this volume will note that neither parents nor educators have reached consensus positions on important issues in education. However, the four central themes which emerge from the experiences of these educational leaders can direct us as we more clearly specify policy alternatives, devise criteria for analyzing these alternatives and provide concise analysis of the political, educational, and economical factors involved. Moreover, these leaders offer us their visions of the practical and policy implications of the current state of education.

Since the United States is dynamic and composed of a conglomeration of social and cultural groups, we will have to live with some disagreement about the philosophy and goals of education. The

1990's provide us with an opportunity to be innovative within the context of our professional tradition of commitment (Raines, this volume). This volume serves as a testament to that tradition as it serves to inform public opinion, research, theory and practice.

Valora Washington

Dean of Faculty
Antioch College
Yellow Springs, Ohio 45387

REFERENCES

Baltes, P. and Brim, O. <u>Lifespan Development and Behavior, Vols. 1-4</u>. (1978-82). New York: Academic Press.

Brookover, W. B. (1985). Can we make schools effective for minority students? <u>Journal of Negro Education</u>, <u>54</u>, (3), 257-268,

Morrison, G. S. (1984). <u>Early Childhood Education Today</u>. 3rd Edition. Columbus, Ohio, Charles E. Merrill Publishing Company.

Washington, V. (1985). Social policy, cultural diversity and the obscurity of Black children. <u>Journal of Educational Equity and Leadership</u>.

Washington, Valora and LaPoint, Velma. <u>Black Children and American Institutions</u>. New York: Garland, 1988.

Washington, Valora and Oyemade, Ura Jean. <u>Project Head Start</u>. New York: Garland, 1987.

Bettye M. Caldwell

AUTOBIOGRAPHICAL SKETCH OF
BETTYE MCDONALD CALDWELL

Bettye McDonald Caldwell, Donaghey Distinguished Professor of Education, College of Education, University of Arkansas at Little Rock.

Family: Husband (6-8-47) Fred T. Caldwell, Jr.; Children (9-18-58) Paul and Elizabeth.

Education:
B.A.   Baylor University, Waco, Texas, 1945
M.A.   State University of Iowa, Iowa City, Iowa, 1946
Ph.D. Washington University, St. Louis, Missouri, 1951

Summary of Professional Experience:
1947-53 and 1955-58. Held a variety of positions at Washington University School of Medicine, including being a trainee in Clinical Psychology, collaborating on research concerned with effects of pre- and perinatal trauma on development of children, development and direction of an evaluation clinic for retarded children and their families, working on gerontological research, and teaching child development at Washington University.

1953-55. Assistant Professor of Psychology, Northwestern University, Evanston, Ilinois.

1959-66. Research Associate, Department of Pediatrics, Upstate Medical Center, State University of New York, Syracuse, NY. Participated in and directed extensive research program concerned with effects of early experience on disadvantaged children. Served as lecturer to freshmen medical students and taught Child Psychology at Syracuse University. During this time, developed and directed the Children's Center, the first infant day care center in America, for the purpose of providing enrichment and stimulation to children from poverty backgrounds. Developed several major research instruments (most notably the HOME Inventory and an observational procedure called APPROACH) as part of this project. The Center served as a model for Head Start and other early enrichment projects and provided training for large numbers of students and future program directors.

1966-69. Dual Professor of Child Development and Education, Syracuse University. Essentially involved a continuation of activities from the previous time period, only with more teaching responsibilities.

1969-74. University of Arkansas at Fayetteville. Teaching done mainly in the Graduate Center in Little Rock. Developed and directed the Kramer Project, a special facility which provided both day care and education for children ranging in age from 6 months to 12 years in a neighborhood public school. Taught courses in Early Childhood and Child Development in the Graduate Center and supervised doctoral candidates.

1974-present. Professor of Education, University of Arkansas at Little Rock. Made Donaghey Distinguished Professor in 1978.

Honors: Alpha Chi, Sigma Xi, Phi Beta Kappa (as graduate). Named Woman of the Year in Greater Little Rock (1970); Teacher of the Year (1972); one of ten Women of the Year (Inspirational and Educational Leadership) by Ladies Home Journal (1976); member of Laureate Chapter of Kappa Delta Pi, limited to 60 leading leaders in education (1977); Alumna of the Year, Baylor University, 1980. Listed in many directories, including Who's Who in America.

Professional Organizations: Greatest activity in Society for Research in Child Development (Governing Board 1975-81) and National Association for the Education of Young Children (President 1982-84).

Related Professional Activities: Member of many national advisory groups (1970 White House Conference on Children, 1980 White House Conference on Families); of official U.S. delegations to professional meetings in other countries (Soviet Union, PRC, India); invited speaker to early childhood groups in many countries; Editor of Child Development (1968-71); Editorial Advisory Board, Johnson & Johnson; member of Child Development Advisory Council, Mattel Toys; Contributing Editor, Working Mother; on many research review panels.

Civic Activities: Director, First Commercial Bank, Little Rock; member of Interim School Board, Little Rock, North Little Rock, and Pulaski County; on many boards of community service organizations.

Publications: Over 100 articles and books dating back to 1951.

VIEWS ON CONTEMPORARY ISSUES

It is an honor to be considered a leader in education and to be asked my views on major issues facing children and families today and in the future. When asked about my roots in this field and the influences which shaped my career, I am sometimes hard put to trace a consistent trajectory from where I began to where I am today. Yet, with a fair amount of wobbling in the arc, I suppose I have stayed pretty much on course.

I cannot remember a time when I was not interested in young children. In fact, I always liked to play with children who were younger than I was -- a habit I was not able to change even after learning, many years later, that "bright" children were suposed to enjoy playing with older children. It may have been because I was both the youngest and smallest child in my class all through school, and in physical activities I did better with younger children. But in church I would always go by the "cradle roll" departments after my own class let out and play with and carry around the babies whose parents would allow this. All through school I loved being given an assignment by my principal to "help out" with the younger children. As a freshman in high school I taught myself, with the aid of a book, to twirl a baton. In the tenth grade, I got my first taste of formal teaching when I began offering classes to large numbers of younger girls who wanted to twirl in the high school band. It was the first -- but by no means the last -- time that I declared myself without benefit of formal training, an "expert", qualified to teach. I was just enough ahead of my pupils to make it work. Without knowing what I was doing, I had solved Montessori's "problem of the match." It worked well for the girls, for the band (which won all sorts of competitions with my corps of majorettes), and for me.

The Right Idea at the Right Time

I had not thought much about my majorette pupils for a long time. But, in reflecting on my assignment to discuss how I became interested in children, I decided that the story was worth relating because it encapsulates whatever success I have had in influencing educational programs for children and support programs for their families. Although twirling does not seem very worthwhile to me now (in college I began to consider it beneath my dignity and stopped abruptly), in the fading years of the Great Depression a group of young girls marching and twirling silver batons clearly met a community need in a small town that enjoyed feeling proud of its young people.

4

In my time on the educational stage, I have made significant contributions in three areas, all of which impacted the field because they met pressing community needs relating to young children and families rather than because they represented major intellectual breakthroughs in the history of ideas. These are:

1. The development of comprehensive infant care and education programs including parent involvement and support.

2. A conceptual reformulation of both early education and day care, recognizing that they are the same service with similar goals, opportunities, and challenges.

3. Advocacy of integrated public school programs providing continuity from early childhood through the elementary years, extending both the school day and school year to accommodate modern patterns of family employment and life style.

In implementing these ideas, I have had enormous amounts of help from thinkers and writers of the past and present (Montessori, Dewey, Hunt, Bloom, Bruner, and many others) and from dedicated and brilliant colleagues (Richmond, Honig, Bradley, Elardo, Thompson-Rountree, and on and on). But I think that, for all of us, the impact of the ideas was due more to their timing than to anything specific that any of us did. We translated the concepts into action at a time in history when the resulting programs clearly met a societal need. And we did so just an eye blink ahead of others who were, unbeknown to us, thinking along the same lines and coming to the same programmatic conclusions.

Infant Care and Education

In 1964, my colleague, Julius B. Richmond, and I launched the Children's Center in Syracuse, New York. Alice Honig, a contributor to this volume, was a vital member of the initial professional staff. The Center represented an attempt to implement some of the major theoretical positions about the importance of early experience, especially with respect to disadvantaged children, that were current at the time. The launching of the program required me, for a second time in my history, to declare myself qualified to do what I was about to do. As there was absolutely no one around who knew anything about infant intervention, I was on safe grounds!

In the years since that project began, the need for quality care and education for infants has increased exponentially. Although

5

statistics become obsolete almost before they can appear in print, at the present time almost one-half of mothers with children younger than three are employed outside the home. This means that quality environments in which these children can spend a significant portion of their early years must be designed and made available to the children and their parents. No matter what developmental theory might imply about the consequences of such services, they are a reality of life for millions of children. This reality mandates the development of programs which will be growth-fostering and the elimination of program characteristics which will militate against the optimal development of children. The need for such services also provides an opportunity to "equalize" early environmental conditions for those children whose natural home environments are lacking in conditions necessary to support development. Designing and operating comprehensive infant care and education programs, trying to influence public opinion about their potential value, and advocating standards of high quality in such programs represent activities which have consumed a great deal of my time and energy over the past 25 years.

Merger of Early Education and Day Care

Trying to persuade people that day care and early childhood education are actually one service has been a cause celebre for me for 25 years. A confession which I do not too often make in public is that I stumbled into day care while trying to develop an early childhood education program for infants. As anything which advocated involvement of infants with adults other than their mothers for even brief periods violated acceptable scientific and humane canons of the period, we were advised to limit our infant enrichment to infants "already in substitute care" -- i.e., day care. Stung by early criticisms of the program as somehow not being educational because it offered day care, I struggled to understand how legitimate and well-intentioned professionals could make a distinction between these fields. I concluded that it was because they were armchair philosophers and that I was the pragmatist who was actually laboring in the vineyard. From my vantage point, I knew that it was impossible to provide "care and protection" -- the hallmarks of day care -- to children without "educating" them, and vice versa. In hundreds of speeches and dozens of articles written over the past 25 years, I have tried to gain adherents to the position that the terms "day care" (or child care, to use its more popular current term) and "education" represent a false dichotomy and that better programs will result when we design comprehensive services that can be utilized for shorter or longer periods of time, depending on the family's daily schedule of activities. Although this conceptualization seems so logical to me that I cannot really understand opposition to it, such resistance is still there in some circles. But the resistance appears to be weakening, primarily as a result of the inexorable march of demographics which make anything other than a comprehensive service obsolete. It is good to live long enough to see one's ideas validated by history.

Comprehensive Schools

The third -- hopefully not the last -- contribution I have made to the field of education is one that is so simple-minded that one might conclude that only a fool would attempt it. And it represents the third time in my history when, as there was no one with relevant experience who could challenge me, I simply declared myself qualified to do what I proposed to do. On the basis of early data from the Syracuse project and from similar early intervention projects conducted around the country, I came to the conclusion that early education needed to be more meaningfully linked with elementary education in order to provide for continuity of support throughout the childhood years. Moving in 1969 to Little Rock, Arkansas -- a city not reknowned for concern for the education of its black and poor children -- I explored with public school officials the possibility of converting an elementary school into an early childhood-elementary facility which would operate year-round and remain open for 12 hours each day in order to accommodate the day care needs of working parents.

The result was the Kramer Project, the professional achievement in my life of which I am most proud. In part because of the high mobility of the families in the Kramer attendance area, and in part because we did a lot of things poorly, the research which underpinned the Kramer effort lacked the elegance and the power found in other intervention programs conducted at that time in different parts of the country. However, enough was learned both in-house and by thousands of visitors to the project to support the position that this model of a comprehensive, extended day and extended month school is the model which most fits the needs of children and families in modern urban society. Kramer, like the Syracuse project, was just a little bit ahead of its time. But the times are catching up with it.

And I have used up my six pages, and then some. Preparing any sort of autobiographical material is rather like doing a needs assessment for an organization. Now I feel that I know what I have

7

done -- and perhaps understand a bit of what I need to do in the future!

SELECTED RECENT PUBLICATIONS

Professor Caldwell has more than 100 publications dating back to 1951 and covering all the areas in which she has worked in her professional career.

<u>1978</u>:

Caldwell, B. M. & Bradley, R. H. Assessing social and emotional development in young children. In Norbert Enzer (ED.), <u>Social and Emotional Development in Young Children</u>. New York: Walker & Co.

Bradley, R. H. & Caldwell, B. M. Screening the environment. <u>American Journal of Orthopsychiatry</u>, <u>48</u>, 114-130.

Bradley, R. H. & Caldwell, B. M. Home environment, learning processes and IQ. In William Frankenburg (Ed.), <u>Developmental Screening</u>. Denver: University of Colorado.

Bradley R. H. & Caldwell, B. M. Home environment, learning processes, and IQ. <u>Mid-South Educational Researcher</u>, <u>6</u>, 5-6.

<u>1979</u>:

Bradley, R. H., Elardo, R., & Caldwell, B. M. Home environment and cognitive development in the first two years: A cross-lagged panel analysis. <u>Developmental Psychology</u>, <u>15</u>, 246-250.

Bradley, R. H. & Caldwell, B. M. Home environment and locus of control. <u>Journal of Clinical Child Psychology</u>, <u>8</u>, 107-111.

Bradley, R. H. & Caldwell, B. M. Home observation for measurement of the environment: a revision of the preschool scale. <u>American Journal of Mental Deficiency</u>, <u>84</u>, 235-244.

Caldwell, B. M. Optimal child-rearing environment. In Jack Westman (Ed.), <u>Child Advocacy: New Professional Roles for Helping Families</u>. New York: Free Press.

Freund, J. H., Bradley, R. H., & Caldwell, B. M. The home environment in the assessment of learning disabilities. <u>Learning Disabilities Quarterly</u>, <u>4</u>, 39-51.

<u>1980</u>:

Caldwell, B. M. Balancing children's rights and parents' rights. In R. Haskins & J. J. Gallagher (Eds.), <u>Care and Eduation of Young Children in America: Policy, Politics, and Social Science</u>. Norwood, NJ: Ablex.

Caldwell, B. M. Assignment on Bleaker Street. In Gertrude J. Williams (Ed.), Children in the Twenty-First Century, Journal of Clinical Child Psychology, Vol. IX, No. 2, pp. 134-144.

Bradley, R. H. & Caldwell, B. M. Home environment, cognitive competence, and IQ among males and females. Child Development, 51, 1140-1148.

Caldwell, B. M. Quo Vadis Familia? University of Arkansas at Little Rock Monograph Series (pp. 76-88). Little Rock, Arkansas.

1981:

Bradley, R. H. & Caldwell, B. M. The HOME Inventory: A validation of the preschool scale for black children. Child Develoment, 52, 708-710.

Caldwell, B. M. (Spring, 1981). Day Care and the Schools. Theory into Practice, Vol. XX, No. 2.

Bradley, R. H. & Caldwell, B. M. (Spring, 1981). Home environment and infant social behavior. Infant Mental Health Journal.

Bradley, R. H., & Caldwell, B. M. Home environment, cognitive processes, and intelligence: a path analysis. In M. Friedman, J. Das, and N. O'Connon (Eds.), Intelligence and Learning. New York: Plenum.

Bradley, R. H. & Caldwell, B. M. Pediatric usefulness of home assessment. In Bonnie Camp (Ed.), Advances in Behavioral Pediatrics (Vol. 2). Greenwich, CT: JAI Press.

1982:

Caldwell, B. M. (May/June). Our Children, Our Resources. Childhood Education.

Caldwell, B. M. & Freyer, M. Day Care and early education. In B. Spodek (Ed.), Handbook of Research in Early Childhood Education (pp. 341-374). New York: Free Press.

Caldwell, B. M. & Bradley, R. H. Screening for handicapping environments. In E. Edgar, N. Haring, J. Jenkins, C. Pious (Eds.), Mentally Handicapped Children. Baltimore: University Park Press.

Caldwell, B. M. Effective strategies for early intervention. In J. Rajalakshmi (Ed.), Nutrition and the Development of the Child (pp. 372-378). Baroda, India: M.S. University of Baroda.

Bradley, R. H. & Caldwell, B. M. The consistency of the home environment and its relation to child development. International Journal of Behavioral Development, 5, 445-465.

Caldwell, B. M. What is quality day care? In P. E. Reilly (Ed.), Education for Development (pp. 26-33). Bophuthatswana: Southern African Association for Early Childhood Education.

Caldwell, B. M. International developments in early childhood education. In P. E. Reilly (Ed.), Education for Development (pp. 18-25). Bophuthatswana: Southern African Association for Early Childhood Education.

1983:

Caldwell, B. M. (Autumn). Child Development and Cultural Diversity. FUTURE (Vol. 8). New Delhi, India: UNICEF House.

Caldwell, B. M. How can we educate the American public about the child care profession? Young Children, 38, 11-17.

1984:

Bradley, R. H. & Caldwell, B. M. The HOME Inventory and Family Demographics. Developmental Psychology, 20, No. 2, 315-320.

Bradley, R. H. & Caldwell, B. M. The relation of infants' environments to achievement test performance in first grade: A follow-up study. Child Development, 55, 803-809.

Bradley, R. H. & Caldwell, B. M. 174 Children: A study of the relation between home environment and mental development in the first five years. In A. Gottfried (Ed.), Home Environment and Early Cognitive Development (pp. 5-56). New York: Academic Press.

Boyd, H. W., Jr. & Caldwell, B. M. The marketing of Early Childhood Programs. Journal of Children in Contemporary Society, 17, No. 2, 3-22.

Caldwell, B. M. & Boyd, H. W., Jr. Effective Marketing of Quality Child Care. Journal of Children in Contemporary Society, 17, No. 2, 25-36.

1986:

Caldwell, B. M. (February). Day Care and the Public Schools -- Natural Allies, Natural Enemies. Educational Leadership, 43, No. 5, 34-39.

Caldwell, B. M. (Spring). Bi-directionality in Education. The Educational Forum, 50, No. 3, 295-307.

Bradley, R. H., Caldwell, B. M., Fitzgerald, J. A., Morgan, A. G., & Rock, S. L. Behavioral Competence of Maltreated Children in Child Care. Child Psychiatry and Human Development, Vol. 16 (3), 171-193.

Bradley, R. H., Caldwell, B. M., Fitzgerald, J. A., Morgan, A. G., and Rock, S. L. Experiences in day care and social competence among maltreated children. Child Abuse and Neglect, Vol. 10, pp. 181-189.

Caldwell, B. M. & Bradley, R. H. Infant Intervention and Social and Cultural Factors. In D. Tamir, T. Brazelton, and A. Russell (Eds), Stimulation and Intervention in Infant Development. London: Freund Publishing House.

Bradley, R. H., Caldwell, B. M., Rock, S. L., & Harris, P. T. (Spring). Early home environment and development of competence. Findings from the Little Rock Longitudinal study. Children's Environments Quarterly, Vol. 3, No. 1, pp. 10-22.

Casey, P., Bradley, R. H., Caldwell, B. M., & Edwards, Diane. (August). Developmental Intervention: A Pediatric Clinical Review. Pediatric Clinics of North America, Vol. 33, No. 4, 899-923.

Caldwell, B. M. Prefessional Child Care: A Supplement to Parental Care. In N. Gunzenhauser & B. Caldwell (Eds.), Group Care for Yong Children. Skillman, NJ: Johnson & Johnson Baby Products Company.

Caldwell, B. M. (June). Day Care and Early Environmental Adequacy. In W. Fowler (Ed.), Early Experience and the Development of Competence. San Francisco: Jossey-Bass.

Caldwell, B. M. (Fall). Helping Children "do unto others." INSTRUCTOR'S ECE Teacher, Special Edition, pp. 5-6.

Caldwell, B. M. Education of Families for Parenting. In M. Yogman & T. Brazelton (Eds.), In Support of Families. Cambridge: Harvard University Press.

1987:

Bradley, R. H. & Caldwell, B. M. Early environment and cognitive competence: The Little Rock Study. Early Child Development Care, 27, pp. 307-341.

Caldwell, B. M. Sustaining Intervention Effects -- Putting Malleability to the Test. In J. Gallagher and C. Ramey (Eds.), The Malleability of Children. Baltimore: Brookes Publishing Co.

Caldwell, B. M. (May). Staying Ahead: The Challenge of Third-Grade Slump. Principal, Vol. 66, No. 5, 10-14.

Book Reviews:

Caldwell, B. M. (1983). A Prototype of Head Start. Review of From 3 to 20: The Early Training Project, by S. Gray, B. Ramsey, and R. Klaus. Contemporary Psychology, 28, No. 6, 474-476.

Books:

Caldwell, B. M. & Ricciuti, H. N. (Eds). (1973). Review of child development research. Vol. 3. Chicago: University of Chicago Press.

Caldwell, B. M. & Stedman, D. J. (Eds.). (1977). Infant education: a guide to helping handicapped children in the first three years. New York: Walker & Company.

Frank, M., & Caldwell, B. M. (Eds). (1985). Marketing and Child Care Programs: Why and How. New York: The Hayworth Press.

Gunzenhauser, N., & Caldwell, B. M. (Eds.). (1986). Group Care for Young Children, Pediatric Roundtable: 12. Skillman, NJ: Johnson & Johnson Baby Products Company.

Caldwell, B. M. (Consulting Editor). (1987). When Others Care for Your Child. Alexandria, VA: Time-Life Books, Inc.

K. Alison Clarke-Stewart

AUTOBIOGRAPHICAL SKETCH OF
ALISON CLARKE-STEWART

A native of Vancouver, Canada, I did my undergraduate work, in psychology and zoology, at the University of British Columbia, and also received a master's degree in psychology from that institution, completing a master's thesis on perceptual learning under the supervision of Richard Tees Kessen and took a Ph.D. in developmental psychology in 1972. My dissertation (later published as an SCRD monograph) was entitled "Interactions between mothers and their young children: Characteristics and consequences." After graduation, I took a position as Assistant Professor in the Department of Education at the University of Chicago. I stayed at the University of Chicago until 1982, when I went to the Center for Advanced Study in the Behavioral Sciences at Stanford for a memorable year. Unable to face returning to another Chicago winter, I then moved to my present position as Professor in the Program in Social Ecology at the University of California, Irvine. Over the years, I have done research and published books and articles in the areas of mother-infant and father-infant interaction, parent education, social and cognitive development in early childhood, day care, divorce, and social policy. Most recently I have been working on a study of children's ability to act as witnesses. To help pay the mortgage for a house in Laguna Beach, I have also written several undergraduate textbooks in developmental psychology. My current interests include infant day-care policy, the consequences of joint custody for parents and children, and the trustworthiness of children in the courtroom.

THE CHANGING AND COMPLEX ISSUES
OF EARLY CHILDHOOD EDUCATION:
A PERSONAL RESEARCH ODYSSEY

The History of early childhood education began for me, and to some extent for this country, just 20 years ago. It was the height of the 1960's. I was a shiny, new graduate student in developmental psychology -- young, fresh, eager -- who found myself quite suddenly in an environment where everyone was fighting against the war in Vietnam and in the War on Poverty. Academic psychologists who had spent their entire professional lives in pristine laboratories were venturing into the messy real world to test their theoretical notions by intervening in people's lives. Promising new programs of social change were springing up everywhere. Hopes were high, spirits infectious. I joined the fight. And the means of fighting I selected was early childhood education.

In the late 1960's, early childhood education was an exciting new idea -- an idea that raised important issues and questions for a developmental psychologist. Two decades later, early education is still an exciting idea and still raises important issues. But those issues, it seems to me, have changed.

In 1967, the key issue in early childhood education seemed to be just how important the earliest years of life are for education. Until that time, formal education generally had been limited to instruction during the school years. In the 1960's, people began suggesting that valuable time was being lost by putting off education until the school years. Some people even questioned whether preschool was early enough to begin early education. There was growing concern that Head Start, a program for 4-year-olds, was not having the longlasting effects that had been expected. As a result, the suggestion was made that what was needed was to begin even earlier, with infants. Either because infancy was a critical period for education or because the effects of education were cumulative, it was asserted, the earlier education started, the better.

In addition to this issue of the timing of early education efforts, the other central issue in the late 1960s was the issue of whether early education is compensatory. People surmised that educational programs for young, poor children could compensate for their depriving conditions at home and give them the kinds of experiences that more privileged middle-class children enjoy, consequently enhancing their development and giving them a better chance of succeeding in school. Whether this was indeed the case was a salient issue for psychologists and educators. To address these two issues, investigators undertook scores of programs for disadvantaged infants, toddlers, and preschoolers.

I was involved in one of those programs (Kessen, Fein, Clarke-Stewart, & Starr, 1975). In our study we hoped to discover not only whether early childhood education is critical and compensatory, but what kind of early childhood program is "best." We randomly assigned subjects to one of six educational conditions (focused on children's social, language, or cognitive development, targeted to mothers,

15

infants, or mother-infant dyads), and we assessed mothers' and infants' behavior extensively before, during, and after our year-and-a-half long program.

By the time we had finished this study in the mid 1970s, we had discovered not which educational curriculum was best, but that early education was more complicated than we had thought. It wasn't just that designing the curricula and doing the research was complicated -- it was that the results were complex. We had expected simple and enlightening results: the language-oriented curriculum would enhance children's language development; the play-oriented curriculum would accelerate their cognitive development; the social curriculum would enrich their social development; the dyadic focus would be superior to the mother-only or child-only focus. What we got, though, was p level soup. Effects on boys were different from effects on girls; effects on children in extended families were different from effects on children in nuclear families; the language curriculum was superior on some measures of intellectual development but not all. There was no simple match between curriculum and outcome; there was no clear advantage of dyadic over monadic curricula; and effects evident after 6 to 12 months of home visiting did not persist until the end of the entire 18-month program.

We made these discoveries at a time when parent-training programs, of which ours was an example, were booming. Because parents could reach children earlier, more extensively, and over longer periods of time and hence extend the principles of early education beyond the program itself, parent education was being promoted as a more effective and economical method of reaching disadvantaged children. There were toy libraries for parents, brief interventions in clinic waiting rooms, home visiting programs, and the most comprehensive program, the Parent-Child Development Centers. According to U. S. Commissioner of Education, Terrell H. Bell (1976), parent education was "the key to effective education," and every child "had the right to a trained parent."

The complex and inconsistent results of our detailed attempts to analyze not just the outcomes of early childhood education, but the process, however, led me to a skeptical view of the parent education "movement" (Clarke-Stewart, 1979). I questioned whether there was a justification for parent education in the findings of basic child development research. Basic research supposedly showed that parents substantially determined their children's development. In fact,

16

as I pointed out, this empirical base was shaky. I questioned the presumed effectiveness of parent education. True, most parent-training programs that had been evaluated had been shown to have positive effects on children's intellectual development over the short run. But most parent programs had <u>not</u> been evaluated. Those that had been evaluated were model programs,and it was unclear how widely their results could be generalized. Moreover, the evaluations of the model programs had been of the simplest sort: pre and post tests of children's IQ, with no randomly assigned control group for comparison. The observed effects of parent-training programs were always modest in size and usually short-lived. Effects on aspects of development other than intelligence had not been assessed. In brief, the effectiveness of parent education was an open question.

There was also the issue of how parent education worked. The underlying assumption of parent educators was that the process consisted of a simple chain of influence from program designer to parent to child. This presumed process, however, was based on a chain of unexamined and, as I pointed out in my review, probably untrue, assumptions.

These assumptions are still untested. Before they could be empirically assessed, it seems, the pressing issues in early childhood education had changed.

The 1970's issue, of the most effective approach to early childhood education, was overshadowed in importance in the 1980s by the issue of the effects -- possibly damaging -- of full-day programs for young children. The number of mothers with preschool children who were employed outside the home had skyrocketed over the previous decade, and concern about the well-being of their children was being expressed. Some speakers took a positive view and suggested that full-time day care was as benign as nursery school, but better. Others, extrapolating -- inappropriately -- from studies of the dire consequences of rearing children in residential institutions, vehemently opposed day care. The issue required investigation of the actual effects of day care on children's development. Such studies were begun, and I joined in the research effort.

Again, I was confronted by unanticipated difficulties in the research and unexpected complexities in the results. It was immediately clear that "day care" is not a uniform entity and that one must look for differential effects depending on the type and quality of

17

day care. Studies, including mine, following this approach generally showed that day care does not harm and may even speed up the development of social and intellectual competence in preschool children if the programs are center-based, with structured educational curricula and small classes, run by well-trained and highly educated teachers (see Clarke-Stewart & Fein, 1983). But the problem was that the studies did not -- perhaps could not -- establish whether these differences were a direct result of the day-care programs themselves or simply reflected self selection of participants. They did not establish the limits of teacher training or class size. They did not provide guidelines to guarantee high quality. They did not reveal (or even search for) individual differences among children in day-care effects.

Today, early childhood education is a broader concept than ever before. It includes many approaches, many targets, many justifications. Today, one of the most important issues is how to tailor programs to people -- how to accommodate programs to the circumstances, values, and goals of particular families and communities and to the needs and characteristics of particular children. Now people are no longer searching for the one best early childhood program. Now they are more aware of individual constraints on development. Now efforts need to be made to maximize the "goodness of fit" between programs and participants.

One group of participants for whom this is true, for example, are infants who are "at risk" -- the infants of teenage mothers and older mothers, single mothers and abusive mothers, infants who are premature, underweight, or have physical defects. These new targets of our educational efforts require a new set of guidelines for educational programs.

So, in fact, do all infants. The fastest growing segment of employed mothers these days is mothers with infants between 3 weeks and 3 months of age. If things continue as they are, soon half of the mothers of infants in this country will be working. The question of what is best -- or what is risky -- for the infants of these working mothers is a major concern of parents and professionals in psychology, education, and child care. It is also a controversial issue -- one which is still far from resolved.

There is an urgent need for researchers to investigate the effects of full-time and part-time day care on infants' development, particularly on their emotional well-being. There is a need to find out whether it makes a difference what kind and quality of day care infants are in. There is a need to develop optimal curricula for infant care. It is impossible to extrapolate to infant care programs from the results of research on curricula in preschool programs, care for infants in hospital nurseries, or maternal care of infants at home. Infant day care is a new field -- one that needs continued program development as well as continued evaluation of outcomes. There is also a need to be concerned about the selection and training of caregivers for infant day-care centers. We need more than fingerprinting and early childhood degrees as criteria for hiring. We need new guidelines for hiring and for training infant care workers in day-care centers. Similarly, we need to investigate how in-home sitters and day-care home providers can be trained or inspired to offer the most satisfactory experiences to their infant charges. We most urgently need to investigate how infant care facilities, whether homes or centers, can be continuously monitored and evaluated. These contemporary issues in early childhood education demand both attention and careful research -- just as those of 10 and 20 years ago did. And I will continue to be picking away at them, searching for a clearer -- although assuredly a more complex -- understanding of how early childhood education can promote young children's development.

PUBLICATION BIBLIOGRAPHY

BOOKS AND MONOGRAPHS:

Fein, G. G. & Clarke-Stewart, K. A. (1972). Day care in context. New York: John Wiley and Sons.

Clarke-Stewart, K. A. (1973). Interactions between mothers and their young children: Characteristics and consequences. Monographs of the Society for Research in Child Development, 38 (6-7, Serial No. 153).

Clarke-Stewart, K. A. (1977). Child care in the family: A review of research and some propositions for policy. New York: Academic Press.

Glick, J., & Clarke-Stewart, K. A. (Eds.) (1978). The development of social understanding. New York: Gardner Press.

Clarke-Stewart, K. A. (1982). Daycare. Cambridge, MA: Harvard University Press, published jointly by Fontana (London). Translated into Italian as L'assistenza diurna ai bambini, published by Armando Armando, Rome. 1984. Translated into Spanish as Guarderias y cuidado infantil, published by Ediciones Morata, Madrid, 1984.

Clarke-Stewart, K. A. & Koch, J. (1983). Children: Development through adolescence. New York: John Wiley and Sons.

Clarke-Stewart, K. A., Friedman, S. & Koch, J. (1985). Child development: A topical approach. New York: John Wiley and Sons.

Clarke-Stewart, K. A. & Friedman, S. (1987). Child and adolescent development. New York, John Wiley and Sons.

Clarke-Stewart, K. A., Perlmutter, M., & Friedman, S. (1988). Lifelong development. New York: John Wiley and Sons.

Clarke-Stewart, K. A. (in preparation). Worlds of childhood. New York: Basic Books.

ARTICLES AND CHAPTERS:

Tees, R. C., & [Clarke-Stewart, K. A.] (1966). Identical figures, exposure time and disappearance phenomena under reduced stimulation conditions. Psychonomic Science, 6, 289-290.

Tees, R. C., & [Clarke-Stewart, K. A.] (1967). Effect of amount of perceptual learning upon disappearances observed under reduced stimulation conditions. Perception and Psychophysics, 2, 565-568.

Tees, R. C. & [Clarke-Stewart, K. A.] (1967). Visual disappearances under simplified stimulus conditions caused by auditory perceptual learning. Perception and Psychophysics, 2, 627-629.

Tees, R. C., & [Clarke-Stewart, K. A.] (1968). Effect of temporal and spatial stimulus relationships in controlled perceptual learning upon disappearances observed under reduced stimulation conditions. Perception and Psychophysics, 3, 337-340.

Clarke-Stewart, K. A. (1976). Variations in home-based early education: Social development. In K. F. Riegel & J. A. Meacham (Eds.), The developing individual in a changing world. Volume 2. Social and environmental issues. Chicago: Aldine.

Clarke-Stewart, K. A. (1977). Dr. White's patent elixir for parents. Review of Education, 3, 101-111.

Clarke-Stewart, K. A. (1978). Recasting the lone stranger. In J. Glick & K. A. Clarke-Stewart (Eds.), The development of social understanding. New York. Gardner Press.

Clarke-Stewart, K. A. (1978). And daddy makes three: The father's impact on mother and young child. Child Development, 49, 466-478.

Clarke-Stewart, K. A. (1979). Evaluating parental effects on child development. In L. Shulman (Ed.), Review of research in education. Volume 6. Itasca, IL: F. E. Peacock.

Clarke-Stewart, K. A. (1978). Popular primers for parents. American Psychologist, 33, 359-369.

Clarke-Stewart, K. A. (1979). The family drama of child development. In T. B. Brazelton & V. C. Vaughn (Eds.), The family: Setting priorities. New York: Science and Medicine Publishers.

Clarke-Stewart, K. A., Vanderstoep, L., & Killian, G. A. (1979). Analysis and replication of mother-child relations at two years of age. Child Development, 50, 777-793.

Clarke-Stewart, K. A. (1980). The father's contribution to children's cognitive and social development in early childhood. In F. A. Pedersen (Ed.), The father-infant-relationship: Observational studies in the family setting. New York: Praeger Special Studies.

Clarke-Stewart, K. A., Umeh, B. J., Snow, M. E., & Pederson, J. A. (1980). Development and prediction of children's sociability from 1 to 2 1/2 years of age. Developmental Psychology, 16, 290-302.

Clarke-Stewart, K. A. (1980). Current issues in mother-child research. Monographs of the Society for Research in Child Development, 45 (6-7, Serial No. 187), 90-105.

Clarke-Stewart, K. A. (1981). Observation and experiment: Complimentary strategies for studying day care and social development. In S. Kilmer (Ed.), Advances in early education and day care. Volume 2. Greenwich, CT: JAI Press.

Clarke-Stewart, K. A. & Hevey, C. M. (1981). Longitudinal relations in repeated observations of mother-child interaction from 1 to 2 1/2 years. Developmental Psychology, 17, 127-145.

Clarke-Stewart, K. A. (1981). Parent education in the 1970's. Educational Evaluation and Policy Analysis, 3, 47-48.

Clarke-Stewart, K. A. (1983). Exploring the assumptions of parent education. In R. Haskins, & D. Adams (Eds.), Parent education and public policy. Norwood, NJ: Ablex Publishing.

Clarke-Stewart, K. A. (1983). The family as a child care environment. In A. S. Skolnick & J. H. Skolnick (Eds.), Family in transition. Boston: Little Brown, 1983.

Clarke-Stewart, K. A., & Fewin, G. G. (1983). Early childhood programs. In P. H. Mussen, M. Haith, & J. Campos (Eds.), Handbook of child psychology, Volume 2, Infancy and developmental psychobiology. New York: John Wiley and Sons.

Clarke-Stewart, K. A. (1984). Programs and primers for child rearing education: A critique. In R. P. Boger, G. E. Blom, & L. E. Lezotte, (Eds.), Child nurturance, Volume 4, Child nurturing in the 1980's. New York: Plenum.

Clarke-Stewart, K. A. (1984). Day care: A new context for research and development. In M. Perlmutter (Ed.), The Minnesota Symposium on Child Psychology. Volume 17. Hillsdale, NJ: Lawrence Erlbaum Associates.

Clarke-Stewart, K. A., & Gruber, C. (1984). Day care forms and features. In R. C. Ainslie (Ed.), The child and the day care setting. New York: Praeger Special Studies.

Clarke-Stewart, K. A. (1987). The social ecology of early childhood. IN N. Eisenberg (Ed.), Contemporary topics in developmental psychology. New York: John Wiley and Sons.

Clarke-Stewart, K. A. (in press). A home is not a school: The impact of environment on development. In M. Lewis, & S. Feinman (Eds.), Social influences and behavior. New York: Plenum.

Clarke-Stewart, K. A. (1987). Predicting child development from day care forms and features: The Chicago study. In D. Phillips (Ed.), Predictors of quality child care. NAEYC Research Monographs, Volume 1.

Clarke-Stewart, K. A., & Bailey, B. L. (submitted). Adjusting to divorce: Why is it easier for men? Journal of Divorce.

Clarke-Stewart, K. A. (in press). Development. In D. A. Bernstein, E. J. Roy, T. K. Srull, & C. D Wickens, Introduction to psychology. Boston: Houghton Mifflin.

Glen Dixon

AUTOBIOGRAPHICAL SKETCH OF
GLEN DIXON

Glen Dixon grew up in Winnipeg, Canada, where he studied the violin and first began teaching in the classroom. After completing a degree in music education in Massachusetts, he studied child development at the Eliot-Pearson Department of Child Study, Tufts University, where he was particularly influenced by the teaching of Dr. Evolyn Pitcher and Dr. Esther Edwards.

Having taught for a dozen years at the preschool and elementary levels, mostly in the Boston and New York areas, he completed his doctoral degree at the University of Georgia and then taught at the University of Texas at Austin before returning to Canada in 1977.

Dr. Dixon is an associate professor in the Department of Visual and Performing Arts in Education in Vancouver. He is also the coordinator of Early Childhood Education and director of the UBC Child Study Centre. In addition, he is currently the Vice-President for Early Childhood in the Association for Childhood Education International, and editor of Canadian Children, the journal of the Canadian Association for Young Children.

He has written articles about various aspects of early education, including teaching in the multicultural classroom, built environment education, esthetic education, educational programs in the Yukon and in Jamaica, and non-deficit approaches to parent involvement. He has also developed programs with new uses of videotape for the observation of children by parents, students and teachers, and his television series, "Observing Children," has been shown several times in Canada.

Besides being recognized for his contributions to curriculum development for young children, in recent years, Dr. Dixon has become well-known for his work with parents as partners in the process of early childhood education. The ANCHOR Project, which he developed at the UBC Child Study Centre, is now being adapted for use across Canada and has drawn international attention.

EARLY CHILDHOOD EDUCATION

How many men who enter the traditionally female field of early childhood education, I wonder, do so by an oblique route. For me, an interest in child development began in high school when, for a time, I was the senior violin student in a music studio in Winnipeg, assigned to teach the beginning students, some of whom were only four years old. But this was to be my only involvement with young children until ten years later. My career took a dramatic turn when I was awarded a scholarship for professional musicians, allowing me to become a graduate student in the Eliot-Pearson Department of Child Study at Tufts University, under the direction of Dr. Evelyn Goodenough Pitcher.

Before I started at Eliot-Pearson, Dr. Pitcher arranged for me to teach in a summer Head Start program. This was my first experience of working in partnership with parents in an effort to provide better opportunities for their children. In fact, much of my work today is still concerned with fostering a reciprocal relationship between teachers and parents. The importance of providing a setting for parents to share their feelings about child-rearing with each other and those working with their children in school, was one of the strong beliefs which Dr. Abigail Eliot passed on to her students at Tufts.

As I entered public school teaching, I found that successful education of young children has more to do with understanding and guidance than with clever design of instructional materials and predetermined instructional techniques. Working in different school systems in New Jersey and New York, I also found marked differences in parent expectations and in the degree of importance that they placed on their own influence regarding their children's education. These experiences taught me always to consider the children in my classroom in the context of their own lives at home and in the community, and the importance of relating the curriculum to this context.

I am dismayed at how frequently early childhood programs still continue to offer classroom activities which have little to do with life outside the school and fail to accommodate the evident variety of children's individual learning styles and patterns. Often these programs pay only lip service to the concerns of parents, without considering that parents are likely to be in the best position to judge their own child's needs. Very young children, of course, are at a particular disadvantage when they have not yet learned (or chosen) to conform to the standardized response which is expected of them in these classrooms.

How to help teachers become more sensitive and responsive to children's behaviors, is a question which has interested me for many years. During the time that I was a doctoral student at the University of Georgia (where I had the good fortune to study the history of early childhood education with Dr. Keith Osborn), I also participated in Dr. Herb Sprigle's "Learning To Learn" program, with the goal of training adults to become more knowledgeable about young children through the use of guided videotape observation.

The advantage of this type of program is that it allows viewers to participate in a shared observation of predictable behaviors, but a large amount of time and expense must be spent in preparing the videotapes. The biggest problem, however, is that the videotapes do not travel well. Since the influence of the cultural context is an integral part of children's behaviors, when these behaviors are shown in isolation, they are inadequately understood by students who are not familiar with the setting in which the videotapes were made.

This became obvious after I had returned home to Canada and joined the Faculty of Education at the University of British Columbia. Videotapes which I had previously used successfully with students could not be used in Vancouver, because viewers here judged the behaviors shown to be foreign and therefore irrelevant to their own work. Nevertheless, I still thought that videotape observation could be used effectively, provided that the program was individualized and the videotapes did not have to be laboriously prepared ahead of time.

During the past five years, as Director of the UBC Child Student Centre (which serves the university as a research facility and model preschool), I have focused much of my own research on a program that I developed for two-year-olds and their parents. This program uses closed-circuit television so that the adults can examine children's behaviors as they occur (without prior editing) in the adjoining classroom. Video observation is complemented by discussion of topics related to home and family life, guided by a leader who has expertise in child develoment and early education. It is important to emphasize, however, that this is a non-prescriptive program in which the parent is recognized as being in the best position to understand the needs of his or her own child.

One aspect of the program now under study is the attitudes of parents towards their children's school activities, and the frame of reference they have towards what constitutes educational growth and success. Many parents appear to have a preconceived agenda which they expect their child to follow. They often want to see recognizable and measurable growth with materials used in specific ways, even in the early weeks of school, placing a burden on the child to perform in a prescribed manner. In fact, performance may be seen as necessary evidence that learning is taking place.

Teachers of young children frequently reinforce these attitudes by giving independent, self-initiated learning less value than group activities and allowing few opportunities for private reflection. Their teaching strategies may be chosen for appropriateness to subject content and classroom schedules, without attempting to match them to individual learning needs. Non-compliance or lack of response to these strategies is often interpreted as immaturity so that the child may be unfairly censured, by parent as well as teacher, for the shortcomings of the school.

In assessing our model program at the UBC Child Study Centre, we believe it to be very successful in providing a bridge between home and school and in lowering anxiety about school entrance and parent-child separation. The parents enrolled appear to become more relaxed and realistic in their expectations and more sensitive in judging the value of their child's activities.

Identified as the ANCHOR Project (answering the needs of children through observation and response), the program provides a foundation for the educational philosophy of the Centre. We have been asked to adapt this project for use in several different settings across Canada, including some where children and/or parents have special needs, and a course is currently being developed to train discussion leaders from other institutions.

This project is just one example of how early childhood education is shifting towards a greater appreciation of the needs of children as individuals. Perhaps we are reaching the point where we can no longer afford the cost of standardized education aimed at a hypothetical child, while too many real children are not being properly served.

PUBLICATION BIBLIOGRAPHY

ARTICLES IN REFEREED JOURNALS:

"Investigating Words in the Primary Grades," Language Arts, 54: 418-422, April, 1977.

"Teaching the Children of the Midnight Sun: A Discussion with Primary-Grade Teachers in the Yukon," Childhood Education, 58 (3): 159-163, 1982.

"Integrating a Built Environment Program Into the Primary Curriculum," The History and Social Science Teacher, 20 (3/4): 75-77, Spring 1985.

"Social Behaviors of Children in a Multicultural Preschool," with Sue Fraser. Accepted for publication TESL Canada Journal, April 1986.

"Suggestions for Teaching Preschoolers in a Multilingual Classroom," with Sue Fraser. Accepted for publication Childhood Education, April 1986.

ARTICLES IN OTHER JOURNALS:

"Built Environment Education for Young Children," Early Childhood Education, 11: 41-46, Summer 1978.

"Planning School Programs for the TV Child," Prime Areas, 21 (3): 28-31, Spring 1979.

"A Visit to Jamaica's Basic Schools," Viewpoint, 15(2): 1-3, 1979.

"Children Learn Grammar Through Colour-Coded Clothesline," Highway One, 3(3): 9-12, 1980.

"Videotapes for Early Childhood Teacher Training," Newsletter - Canadian Education Association, 330: 5, February-March, 1981.

"Some Guidelines for Planning a Kindergarten Music Program," Early Childhood Education, 14(1): 19-24, Spring 1981.

"Young Children Learn Writing Watching Teacher as Model," Highway One, 7(3): 41-43, 1984.

"Sexsmith ESL Demonstration Preschool," Canadian Jounal of Research in Early Childhood Education, 1(1), Spring 1985.

"A Preschool Program for Two-Year-Olds and Parents." Accepted for publication, Early CHildhood Educaton Council Journal (Alberta), Spring 1986.

"The Changing World of the Child," Canadian Children, 11(1), Fall 1986.

"From the Editor," Canadian Children, 12 (1), Spring 1987.

"From the Editor," Canadian Children, 12 (2), Fall 1987.

"Extending Art Experiences in the Preschool Classroom," with Pat Tarr, OMEP Journal, Fall 1987, in press.

"Exploring the Built Environment with Young Children," chapter in Pouring the Foundations: A Guide to Built Environment Education. Vancouver: Canadian Society for Education Through Art, 1987.

CURRICULUM MATERIALS:

"Music." Booklet in series. In: G. Browne (ed.), Day Care for School-Agers. Austin, Texas: Texas Department of Human Resources, 1977.

Our Built Environment. Richmond, British Columbia: School District #38, 1979.

"Observing Children." Manual for telecourse EDYC 438, course author, 10 lessons. Vancouver: University of British Columbia - Distance Education Office, 1986.

"Modern Theories of Early Childhood." Manual for telecourse EDYC 336, course author, 12 lessons. Vancouver: University of British Columbia - Distance Education Office, 1987.

Joe L. Frost

AUTOBIOGRAPHICAL SKETCH OF
JOE L. FROST

Joe Frost was born and reared in the Ouachita Mountain area of Arkansas. He graduated from Waldron, Arkansas, High School and attended Oklahoma State University and the University of Maryland before receiving a doctorate in elementary education and child development at the University of Arkansas. His teaching experience includes primary, elementary and junior high levels and demonstration teaching with Head Start and nursery school children. From public school, he moved to university teaching at the University of Arkansas, Iowa State University, University of California at Davis, and the University of Florida. He is presently Catherine Mae Parker Centennial Professor of Curriculum and Instruction in the program of early childhood education at the University of Texas at Austin.

Dr. Frost has lectured in most states, Canada, Mexico, Europe and Asia. He has authored and edited twelve textbooks and numerous articles and research reports. The Disadvantaged Child, co-edited with Glenn Hawkes, was selected by Pi Lambda Theta as one of the outstanding education books for 1966. His most popular book, Early Childhood Education Rediscovered, has been adopted by colleges and universities in all 50 states and in 20 foreign countries. His most recent books are: Children's Play and Playground. (Allyn and Bacon, Inc., 1979) and When Children Play (Association for Childhood Education International, 1985).

Dr. Frost participates in several professional organizations concerned with young children. He is Past-President of the Association of Childhood Education International and is presently U.S.A. Representative to the International Playground Association. His current research interests are children's play and play environments and family relations.

EDUCATIONAL REFORMS
AND THE
POWER OF POLITICS

During my junior year in college, our savings were exhausted; and my wife and I were on the verge of dropping out and returning to work when Professor Lena Rexinger told us of the National Defense Education Act, which provided low interest loans to college students. That legislation kept two certain dropouts in school. Thus, I saw very early, even before earning a college degree, the power of politics in education and society at large. Professor Rexinger became, perhaps, the most influential professional in our lives. Having studied at Columbia Teachers College, when it was the place to go, she was thoroughly grounded in the views of such pioneers as John Dewey, William Kilpatrick and Patty Smith Hill. Her life and teaching were exemplars of "democracy in action" and "learning by doing." To this time, I have found no superior substitute for these basic educational tenets.

In the early 1960's, while a graduate student, I spent portions of three summers at interinstitutional seminars in child development sponsored by the University of Michigan and seven other universities with strong programs in child development. Each university sent faculty members and students to the institutes. The sessions were intense as fledgling students observed almost reverently the intellectual, witty faculty combatants dissecting major issues in child development, and, occasionally, one another.

Having arrived at the first institute with ideas of possibly publishing a paper in the Proceedings, I sought and received a great deal of personal assistance from the faculty. Brian Hughes and Warren Ketcham of the University of Michigan and Anton Brenner of the Merrill Palmer Institute posed challenges and provided support that established my scholarly interest for almost a decade. My lofty goals revolved around the needs of children in poverty. Having grown up poor (without ever knowing it) in the beautiful Ouchita Mountains of Arkansas, there resulted a natural inclination, I suppose, to study the familiar. By 1966, I had completed a doctoral dissertation at the University of Arkansas about the school achievement of welfare recipient children, secured an assistant professorship in child development at Iowa State University and co-edited The Disadvantaged Child with my department chairman, Glenn Hawkes.

This book changed my life. It was selected by Pi Lambda Theta as one of the outstanding education books of 1966. The content was timely since publication coincided with the initiation of President Johnson's Great Society Programs in Education. Schools and agencies, faced with unparalleled need to respond to this national call for action, turned to every available resource for help in planning, training, research and program implementation. The Disadvantaged Child made me an "overnight expert" and the remainder of the 1960's was a whirlwind of activity.

In the summer of 1965, Iowa State University was the recipient of one of the initial training grants for prospective Head Start teachers. With the incomparable planning skills of one of our faculty members, Marilyn Smith (now Executive Director of the NAEYC), and the skillful assistance of Glenn Hawkes, Bruce Gardner, Damaris Pease and Joseph Shea, we helped give birth to the revolutionary Head Start concept. I am indebted to these people for including me in their work.

With the initiation of Head Start, a new and badly needed approach emerged to compensate for the effects of poverty on children of all ethnic backgrougns. From its beginning, Project Head Start represented the most promising, and at the same time, the most exciting educational innovation of our times. Over the next few years, numerous studies, particularly the Westinghouse Report, appeared to cast doubt on the efficacy of early education for poverty children, but those who worked closely on the firing line, in the centers for children, knew differently. On opening day in rural and inner city centers, we saw the scaly skin, sunken cheeks, lifeless hair, blackened teeth and protruding bellies of malnourished kids and learned first-hand of their educational deficiencies. We were unable to recognize many of these same chidlren on a return visit just a few weeks later because of their improved physical appearance and vitality; we knew that Head Start was successful from health benefits alone, not to mention the intellectual and social benefits. Our beliefs were confirmed almost two decades later with the publication of the long-term early childhood intervention studies.

Moving from child development to an education college, at the University of Texas at Austin in 1966, posed no particular dilemma since my training encompassed both fields. There are, however, basic philosophical and practical differences which, I believe, create an almost impenetrable buffer zone for children near the age of school entry. The relative absence of training in child development for elementary teachers results in curricula oriented to structure and content with limited emphasis upon developmental processes. The process orientation of those trained in child development presents an opposing dilemma. Future programs must strike a sensible balance.

During the next few years, I became deeply immersed in the school integration struggle and had many opportunities to see discrimination in its many forms. I learned that you don't have to be black or brown to be discriminated against, although this helps - you need merely to be poor. The poverty area schools of Texas - the central cities of Houston and Dallas, the rural Rio-Grande Valley - saw children from shanties attending school in ramshackle, antiquated, stuffy buildings, taught by ill-prepared teachers using limited, out-of-date materials and equipment. It was years later that court action and legislation forced integration and, more recently, equalization funding for poor school districts. But politics give and politics take away. To cite a specific case, after years of legal actions leading to school integration in the Austin, Texas Public Schools, the local School Board voted, in 1987, to re-segregate the elementary schools of the district!

My work in school integration and Head Start took me to various black college campuses and major inner city and rural areas. I spent long hours in automobiles traveling from airports to schools with black and Mexican-American leaders. I learned not merely from their words but from their general demeanor - frustrations, hesitations, aggressiveness, resignation, subtle meanings - of the despair inherent in enforced second-class citizenship. My professional associates in Head Start learned this, too. I shall never forget Keith Osborn (University of Georgia) standing before an auditorium filled with college faculty and students, tears dropping from his face, relating his experiences in a Mississippi Head Start center for black children that had just been burned to the ground by whites.

Similarly, I shall never forget an overwhelming experience in Alexandria, Louisiana, where I was invited to address the all-black Louisiana Education Association. As the old propeller-driven Trans Texas Airlines plane circled the moon-reflected swampland searching for a tiny airstrip, I suffered misgivings about sharing the speaking responsibilities with Martin Luther King, Jr. In the dimly lit auditorium, filled with black faces, I followed a Baptist minister from New Orleans. He brought the audience to near-frenzy with passion and unbounded energy, and we all stood (one white face - mine) and sang "Let My People Go". Then it was my turn. I did tolerably well, partly due, I

34

suppose, to my childhood memories of fundamentalist church services, but largely due to my naivete and the blacks' deep reverence for Dr. King, and through social interactions with whites in the area, of their unfounded mistrust and fear of him. Prejudice, in its many forms, is the antithesis of education, and its destruction must continue to be a dominant theme in the socialization and schooling of young children. Similarly, poverty is an ally of discrimination. Society must pay whatever price to ensure the dissolution of permanent under-classes through tolerance, enlightenment through education and democratic legislative processes.

Primarily because of my work in Head Start and continuing research on poverty, I was convinced that early childhood education was a key element in overcoming the effects of poverty. Early Childhood Education Rediscovered, published in 1968, was quickly adopted by colleges and universities throughout the English-speaking world and led to the inevitable array of opportunities for speaking, writing and research and development. Work in Head Start was supplemented by working with agencies, such as the regional educational development laboratories, in establishing pilot, experimental, early childhood programs for poverty children. All too frequently, the central issue revolved around appropriate training/education of teachers, the proper foci for curriculum (play, academics, etc.) and the influence of families on the educational success of their children. These three issues dominated my professional career to the present time.

In 1976, a doctoral student, Barry Klein, and I were co-teaching a college class for teachers at the Region XIII Education Service Center in Texas. During our deliberations about the role of play and play environments in the development of children, the class requested that we visit a "good" playground. We searched throughout Central Texas and could not find a "good" one. Consequently, the class designed and built one with children in a migrant school in Lockhart, Texas. In rapid succession, Barry and I published Children's Play and Playgrounds. I initiated a course on the subject at the University of Texas, established a research project and began to build and redevelop playgrounds. These initial activities have since led to study and involvement in several countries.

Play is a critical process in child development, essential in cognitive, emotional, social, moral and motor development. Historically, theories and practice held that play is trivial and inconsequential. The rapidly growing body of research producing evidence contrary to long-held views is leading to a play and play environment movement of considerable importance to education.

With respect to play environments, there are two fundamental practical issues which must continue to be addressed by future researchers and practitioners: 1) how can we best utilize play as a vehicle for development and 2) how can we best assure the safety of children during play?

Presently, one American child is injured on a playground every two minutes. Most serious injuries and fatalities can be prevented by the application of relatively simple safety principles. The International Association for the Child's Right to Play/U.S.A. is presently assuming major leadership roles in ensuring that the above concerns be addressed and resolved.

At the present time, American schooling, according to various national reports, is involved in an "education crisis." Children, the reports say, are unruly and failing in school. Essentially, they believe the schools that enroll children and those that train teachers are to blame. Consequently, politicians, education agencies and administrators are jumping through hoops to establish "educational reforms." These typically include focus on academics, increased time in school, competency testing for both students and teachers and early childhood education. The ultimate fall from grace by teachers of teachers was the decision of the Special 1987 Texas Legislature to outlaw all undergraduate education degrees in the State of Texas, beginning with the graduating class of 1991. Undoubtedly, other states will follow Texas' lead and some, as saner heads prevail, will probably reverse their decisions in the future, particularly those influencing early childhood education. Education, like the stock market, moves in cycles, frequently unpredictable and illogical.

Only one of the major national reforms, expansion of programs in early childhood education, has a substantial research base. A fundamental issue in this context is cause. It is assumed that because children are failing, the teachers and teachers of teachers are at fault. The research, supporting a radically different conclusion, is far more compelling. Children are in trouble primarily because the American family base and, consequently, the moral base of education has eroded. This family base includes variables of divorce, poverty, television, drugs, etc. and is extensively documented. The current dominant emphasis upon reforming the school, without equivalent attention to reforming the family, will be one of our greatest historical disappointments. The simple, unalterable fact is that children who arrive at school from disrupted families will continue to have trouble in school - despite the reforms. History will judge our current politicians harshly for failing to recognize this.

By submitting one vote, a politician in the right position can exert greater influence on the welfare of children in one day than most professional educators can influence in a lifetime. This is not meant to deny the power of teachers in the lives of one or of many children but to admit and bring into question the almost overpowering influence of politics, both good and bad, in my chosen profession.

SELECTED BIBLIOGRAPHY

BOOKS:

(with Glenn R. Hawkes). The Disadvantaged Child: Issues and Innovations. Boston: Houghton Mifflin, 1966, 445pp.

Issues and Innovations in the Teaching of Reading. Chicago: Scott, Foresman & Co., 1967, 359pp.

Early Childhood Education Rediscovered. New York: Holt, Rinehart and Winston, 1968, 47pp.

(with Thomas Rowland). Curricula for the Seventies: Early Childhood Through Early Adolescence. New York: Holt, Rinehart and Winston, 1969, 454pp.

(with Thomas Rowland). The Elementary School: Principles and Problems. Boston: Houghton Mifflin, 1969, 567pp.

(with Glenn R. Hawkes). The Disadvantaged Child: Issues and Innovations. 2nd ed. Boston: Houghton Mifflin, 1970, 499pp.

(with G. Thomas Rowland). Compensatory Programming: The Acid Test of American Education. Dubuque: William C. Brown, 1971, 148pp.

Revisiting Early Childhood Education. New York: Holt, Rinehart and Winston, 1973, 548pp.

(with D. R. Rogers). How to Plan for Effective Teaching: A Programmed Text. Austin: University of Texas (mimeographed), 1974, 248pp.

(with Joan Kissinger). The Young Child and the Educative Process. New York: Holt, Rinehart and Winston, 1976, 390pp.

(with Barry Klein). Children's Play and Playgrounds. Boston: Allyn and Bacon, Inc., 1979, 1983.

(with Sylvia Sunderlin). When Children Play. Washington, D. C.: Association for Childhood Education International, 1985, 355pp.

(with research staff). U. S. Survey of Public School Playgrounds, American Alliance for Leisure and Recreation, in press.

REPORTS AND MONOGRAPHS:

(with Carole Honstead). "The Developmental Psychology of Jean Piaget." Prepared for the Minnesota Mathematics and Science Teaching Project. Summer, 1966.

"Educational Media and the Inhuman Condition." Prepared for the Educational Media Council, Incorporated. December, 1966.

(with staff). Preparing Teachers of Disadvantaged Children. Austin, Texas: Southwest Educational Development Laboratory, 1968.

"Effects of an Enrichment Program on the School Achievement of Rural Welfare Recipient Children." Presented at AERA, Chicago, February, 1968.

"A Two-year Analysis of the West Orange-Cove Early Childhood Program." West Orange-Cove Consolidated Independent School District, 1969.

(with Geneva Hanna Pilgrim). "Effects of a Diagnostic Reading Program on the Achievement of Drop-out Youth." The University of Texas at Austin, 1969.

"Early Childhood Development in Texas: A State in Need of Union." College of Education, University of Texas, Austin, 1972, 13pp. (mimeograph).

(with staff). Report of the Dean's Task Force for Curriculum Development. College of Education, University of Texas, Austin, 1972, 106pp.

"Some Behavioral Science Implications for Developing Literacy through Family and School Influences." College of Education, University of Texas, Austin, 1972, 16pp. (mimeograph).

(with H. Scace). A Survey of Pre-Kindergarten, Kindergarten, First and Second Grades of the San Felipe-Del Rio Consolidated Independent School District. Austin: Management Services Associates, Inc., 1974, 46pp.

(with E. M. Bernal, G. R. Neibuhr, and G. Zamora). Teacher's Television Guide to Carrascolendas. Austin: KLRN-TV, The Southwest Public Broadcasting Council, 1974, 45pp.

(with E. M. Bernal, G. R. Neibuhr and G. Zamora). Theoretical Bases and Program Design for Carrascolendas: 1974 Season. Austin: KLRN-TV, The Southwest Texas Public Broadcasting Council and the University of Texas at Austin, 1974, 81pp.

(with staff). "Looking at Austin's Children." A Survey of Childhood Needs. Austin: The Austin Independent School District and the Hogg Foundation, 1975, 133pp.

(with L. Iscoe). Carrascolendas, the 500 Series: Television Teachers Guide. Austin: KLRN-TV, The Southwest Public Broadcasting Council, 1975, 55pp.

(with staff). Theoretical Bases and Program Design for Carrascolendas: 1975 Season. Austin, KLRN-TV, The Southwest Public Broadcasting Council, 1975, 85pp.

(with Libby Vernon). Development of a Play Environment. Austin: Texas Education Agency, 1978.

Evaluation of the Region VI Head Start Resource Management Institute. Lubbock: Texas Tech University, 1979, 35pp.

(with Rebecca Barrera). Places to Learn Under the Sun. San Antonio: Intercultural Development Research Association, 1979, 74pp.

Commentary: Public Playground Equipment. Consumer Product Safety Commission, Washington, D. C. 1980, 61pp.

(with EDAW Associates). U. S. Army Technical Manual for Children's Play Environments. Atlanta, EDAW Associates, 1984.

(with faculty and staff). Department of Curriculum and Instruction Graduate Survey. University of Texas, Austin, 1985, 117 pp.

CHAPTERS AND SECTIONS:

"A Teacher Appraisal of Living and Learning at the University of Arkansas Training School." Collected Papers of the Inter-Institutional Seminar in Child Development. The Edison Institute, 1962.

"Current Trends in Mathematics." Collected Papers of the Inter-Institutional Seminar, 1963.

(with Glenn R. Hawkes). Adjusting the School Program to the Needs of the Disadvantaged Child." Collected Papers of the Inter-Institutional Seminar in Child Development. The Edison Institute, 1965.

"Language Development in Children." Chapter I in Pose Lamb (ed.), Language Arts for Elementary Schools. Dubuque: William C. Brown, 1967.

"Current Programs in Early Childhood Education." In Proceedings of the Florida Early Childhood Conference. University of South Florida, 1972.

"Application of Structure-Process Theory to the Teaching of Reading." In The Language Arts in the Elementary School: A Forum for Focus, M. L. King, R. Emans, and P. J. Cianciolo (eds.). Urbana, Illinois: National Council of Teachers of English, 1973, pp. 305-318.

"Some Behavioral Science Implications for Developing Literacy Through Family and School Influences." Proceedings: National Conference on Bilingual Education. Austin, Texas: Dissemination Center for Bilingual/Bicultural Education, 1973, pp. 81-88.

"Curriculum Development for Early Childhood." In Proceedings of the Regional Workshops for Early Childhood Education. Charleston: West Virginia Department of Education, 1973, pp. 25-27.

"Issues and Concerns in Early Childhood." In Proceedings: State of Florida Early Childhood Conference. Florida: University of South Florida, 1973, pp. 57-76.

"Beyond Competency Based Teacher Education." In Toward Preparing the Effective Teacher. College of Education, The University of Texas at Austin, 1974.

(with Michael L. Henniger). "Suggested Educational Equipment and Materials for an Infant Group." In M. D. Cohen (ed.), Selecting Educational Equipment and Materials for School and Home. Washington: Association for Childhood Education International, 1976, pp. 40-46.

(with Monroe Cohen, ed.). Developing Programs for Infants and Toddlers. Washington, D. C.: Association for Childhood Education International, 1977.

Educating Teachers for the 1980's: Toward A New School. Chapter I in Klein, B., Collier, J., Jarrett, O., and D. Ulrici (eds.) Innovative Practices in Teacher Education: Preservice Through Inservice, 1977, 1-15pp.

"Toward An Integrated Theory of Play." In J. Boswell (ed.) Proceedings of the Association for Childhood Education International and Brigham Young University National Conference on Child Development. Washington, D. C. ACEI (in press, 21 pp.).

(with EDAW Associates). U. S. Army Technical Manual: Planning and Design of Children's Outdoor Play Environments. EDAW Associates, 1984, 275pp.

(with Sheila Campbell). The Effects of Playground Type on the Cognitive and Social Play Behaviors of Grade Two Children. In When Children Play. J. L. Frost and S. Sunderlin (eds.). Washington, D. C.: Association for Childhood Education International, 1985.

(with Sheila Campbell). Equipment Choices of Primary-Age Children on Conventional and Creative Playgrounds. In When Children Play. J. L. Frost and S. Sunderlin (eds.). Washington, D. C.: Association for Childhood Education International, 1985.

"Children's Playgrounds: Research and Practice." In Greta Fein and Mary Rivkin (Eds.) The Young Child at Play. Reviews of Research, Volume 4. Washington, D. C.: National Association for the Education of Young Children, 1986.

"Planning and Using Children's Playgrounds." In Judy McKee, (Ed.) Play: Working Partner of Growth. Wheaton, Md. Association for Childhood Education International, 1986.

ARTICLES AND ABSTRACTS.

"Welfare Children and Academic Achievement." Association for Research on Growth Relationships, Journal, November, 1964.

"Educating Disadvantaged Children." Journal of the Arkansas Education Association, September, 1964.

"Effects of Enrichment Program on Personality Development of Disadvantaged Chldren." Childhood Education, December, 1968.

(with Betty Frost). "The Difference that Teaching Makes." Grade Teacher. December, 1966.

"Time to Teach." Texas Outlook, October, 1968.

(with Jo Nell James and Lewis F. James). Project for Teachers of Disadvantaged Children." The Southern Journal of Educational Research, 2:157-174, April, 1968.

"Early Childhood Education: The Nature of Educational Objectives." Educational Leadership, 1971.

"Worries Teachers Should Forget." Research in Education, October, 1973, ED-077-576 (abstract).

"Family and School Centers of Learning for Young children." Research in Education, October, 1973, ED-077-572 (abstract).

"Issues and Concerns in Early Childhood Education." Research in Education, October, 1973,ED-077-470 (abstract).

(with J. B. Kissinger). "Issues in Early Childhood Education." Lutheran Education, 1974, 109, 284-294.

"At Risk." Childhood Education, 1975, 51 (6), 298-304.

"Childhood 1776-1976: What Now?" Dimensions, Little Rock: Southern Association for Children Under Six, 1976, 4(4) 82-85, 104-105.

"European Influences on American Play Environments." Texas Association for the Education of Young Children, Newsletter, 1978, 4(3), 1, 7-8.

(with Eric Strickland). "Equipment Choices of Young Children During Free Play." Lutheran Education, September, 1978.

(with Michael L. Henniger). "Making Playgrounds Safe for Children and Children Safe for Playgrounds." Young Children, 34, 5 (1979), 23-30. Reprinted in Dorothy W. Hewes (Ed.) Administration: Making Programs Work for Children and Families, Washington, D. C.: National Association for the Education of Young Children, 1979, 101-108.

"Long-Term Effects of Early Intervention." Dimensions, 8, 2(1980).

"Effects of Day Care on Young Children." Dimensions, 8, 4(1980).

"Free to Be: The Arts and Child Development." Childhood Education, 57, 2 (1980).

"Viewpoints Promoting Communication." Language Arts, 57 (1980) 599-600.

(with Michael Henniger and Eric Strickland). "X-Rated Playgrounds: Issues and Development." Journal of Health, Physical Education, Recreation and Dance. 53 (1982) 72-77. (Reprinted in Recreation, Alberta Canada. 3, April, 1984.).

"Toward an Integrated Theory of Play." Resources in Education, Urbana, Illinois: ERIC PS 0148491, Clearinghouse on Elementary and Early Childhood Education, 1985.

"Safety and Playability in Play Environments." Beginnings, 2 (1985) 11-14.

(with Betty S. Wagner). "Assessing Play and Exploratory Behaviors of Infants and Toddlers," Journal of Research in Childhood Education. 1 (1986), 27-36.

(with Mary K. Dodge). "Children's Dramatic Play: Influence of Thematic and Nonthematic Settings." Childhood Education, 62 (1986), 166-170.

"History of Playground Safety in America", Children's Environments Quarterly, 2 (1985) 13-23.

"Children in A Changing Society: Frontiers of Challenge." Childhood Education, 62 (1986) 242-249.

John I. Goodlad

AUTOBIOGRAPHICAL SKETCH OF
JOHN I. GOODLAD

Education and Degrees:
1939 - Teaching Cert.   Vancouver (Canada) Normal School
1945 - B. A.   University of British Columbia
1946 - M.A.   University of British Columbia
1949 - Ph. D.   University of Chicago

Honorary Degrees:
1967 - L.H.D.   National College of Education
1968 - L.H.D.   University of Louisville
1974 - LL.D.   Kent State University
1976 - LL.D.   Pepperdine University
1982 - D.Ed.   Eastern Michigan University
1982 - L.H.D.   Southern Illinois University
1983 - LL.D.   Simon Fraser University
1984 - L.H.D.   Bank Street College of Education

Honors: Sophomore prize; Dean's list; B.A. first class; graduate fellowship; Kappa Phi Kappa Fellow, 1946-47; Ford Foundation Fellow, 1952-53.

Positions:
Canada:
Teacher, Surrey Schools, British Columbia (including one-room, eight-grade school)
Principal, Surrey Schools, British Columbia
Director of Education, Provincial Industrial School for (Delinquent) Boys, British Columbia (12 grades).

United States:
Consultant in Curriculum, Atlanta (Georgia) Area Teacher Education Service, 1947-49
Associate Professor, Emory University and Agnes Scott College, 1949-50
Professor and Director, Division of Teacher Education, Emory University, and Director, Agnes Scott College-Emory University Teacher Education Program, 1950-56
Professor and Director, Center for Teacher Education, University of Chicago, 1956-60
Director, Corinne A. Seeds University Elementary School, University of California, Los Angeles, 1960-84

Professor, Graduate School of Education, University of
California, Los Angeles, 1960-85
Director of Research, Institute for Development of Educational
Activities, Inc., 1966-82
Dean, Graduate School of Education, University of California,
Los Angeles, 1967-83
Director, Laboratory in School and Community Education,
Graduate School of Education, University of California, Los
Angeles, 1981-84
Visiting Professor, University of Washington, 1983-85
Distinguished Visiting Professor, Brigham Young University,
1983-85
Professor, College of Education, University of Washington, 1985-
present

APPLES, DIAMONDS, AND GLUE*

*(The locale of my schooling was southwestern British Columbia,
where schooling was and is not significantly different from school just
across the boundary shared with the state of Washington.)

Back in the days when newspaper "comics" were comical, I
enjoyed the strip, "Salesman Sam". Sam's favorite hangout was a
small general store where goods were displayed in bulk and in barrels,
the contents of each identified by protruding signs. My favorite
recollection is of three such barrels, one labelled APPLES, another
DIAMONDS, and the third GLUE. The image stays with me and often
comes up sharply on my mental television screen when I think about
schools and school reform.

Growing up, I went to just three schools -- two eight-grade
elementaries and one four-year high school. In retrospect, I realize that
all three were rather small. With one class per grade crowded into
small rooms, the first (in two buildings) could not have enrolled more
than 250 students. The principal taught full-time. The second, one of
the largest in the district, enrolled perhaps 350 students and, again, the
principal taught at least most of the time. With an entering class of
about 140 and some atttrition, the high school probably was in the 400
to 500 range. The principal taught mathematics.

All three environments were, shall we say, intimate. We knew our classmates well, even though we split off into closer, friendship ties when school was out. We knew our schoolmates, too, especially the soccer or baseball heroes, the bullies, and, yes, the bookworms. The principal was highly visible -- throwing out the soccer ball at recess time, showing up unexpectedly when one was doing what one knew not to do, exchanging a class with the teacher of a lower grade (the principal always symbolized power and status by teaching the eighth grade of the elementary school) so that younger students got to see him (nearly always a "him") up close. The janitor (the word "custodian" came later) was equally visible (as was his dog) and master of his domain of furnace room, hallways, basements, stairwells, and even playgrounds.

Field trips were a regular occurrence in the primary grades. The route often took us briefly through the teacher's home where we stopped for cookies. When the circus was in town, there was a day off and a free ticket for anyone whose parent so requested. Yet, school work was intense, as were one's feelings about "good" and "bad" teachers. I hated the music teacher who once cracked me across the head with his baton, and I dislike to this day "Peel's View-Haloo" (the spelling is strictly phonetic), the song we were murdering at the time. But I would have gone over the Berlin Wall for Mr. Terry, my fifth-grade teacher.

Like our older brothers and sisters, we often spoke unkindly of school, but we always were both curious and excited about re-assembling with classmates after the long summer intermission. Each school had its own character, each a little different from the other -- the same but different. I shifted from the first to the second elementary school at the age of nine, several weeks after the fall opening, with the usual uncertainty and even fear. But I was well enough integrated into the new school's culture by Halloween to be tricking and treating with a cohort group and beaten up the next day by the school bully because I had been foolish enough the previous evening to shoot his younger brother with my peashooter. The memories of school are more of walking to and from recess, noon hour, and after-school sports than they are of reading, writing, and arithmetic, but the whole comes together as school and how it dominated my life from age six to just before my seventeenth birthday. Apples, diamonds, and glue, indeed, but all in the same barrel.

From the vantage point of more than four decades as an educator, I see schools then and schools now within the context of a larger ecosystem. Out of nostalgic affection, it would be easy to argue that our schools have gone to hell in a bucket. Some undoubtedly have. But so has the larger context surrounding most schools, in the sense that quite different supporting circumstances now prevail. That long, educative walk home in the dusk of winter is no long safe. Only in the smallest towns do parents and their child's teacher chat over their purchases and know Sam, the general supplier of what they buy. Much more infrequently do older brothers and younger siblings leave a trail in the same school (unless it's private). Few of my classmates came from families with first languages other than English and, when they did, their parents spoke English, too. Teachers hesitate to take field trips today, given the problems of permissions, transportation, and possible lawsuits. Perhaps a third of today's children have a parent free to take them to the circus on a school day. And the diversity of today's high school student population presents challenges far beyond those of yesteryear.

There have been worrisome changes inside the educational system itself. There are far more larger schools. The evidence regarding the comparative advantages of small and large schools is not in and probably will remain inconclusive for years. Yes, up to a certain point, larger high schools can offer more subjects (e.g., more foreign languages) and more extracurricular activities. But research suggests greater curricular sloppiness (e.g., in regard to electives offered) and fewer tough decisions about what is worth learning. And research shows that the same, not different, students tend to load up on extracurricular activities when more are available. Our own research shows closer relations between parents and teachers, stronger beliefs on the part of parents that they know what their children's schools are doing, and greater teacher and parental satisfaction generally in the smallest schools in our sample. One major effort to draw implications from research, worldwide, on school size, led to the conclusion that whatever financial and curricular advantages accompany increasing school size, they rapidly fade out when the enrollment exceeds 400, 600, and 800 for elementary, middle, and high schools, respectively. These figures are comparable to my own conclusions. In England, headmistresses of Infant Schools (enrolling children from the age of five through seven) express dismay over the size of our schools and concern when their own enroll more than 250 children.

The closeness of families and schools and their teachers when I

47

was a child probably was a correlate of small school size and of the relatively higher esteem with which teachers were regarded in the community. Goodness knows, it was not salary. As best as I am able to determine, my teachers brought home about $5.00 a day for 180 days of the year. Given the irregularity of employment, carpenters and brick layers probably brought home their $8.00 and $12.00 per day, respectively, for the same 180 days annually. My annual nine-month salary (with little hope of employment for the remaining three months), as a rural teacher in charge of an eight-grade, one room school, a year after graduation from high school, was $780.00.

The second factor in teachers' esteem grew out of the fact that teachers (with a high school diploma and a year in a normal school required for elementary school teachers) had more schooling than did most parents and others in the community. High school teachers were more schooled than almost everyone. More important, they were numbered among a relatively small percentage of the population going beyond an eight-grade common school. Consequently, they did know how to read, write, spell, and figure at a reasonably high level and usually carried with them a relatively rich historical and literary background. Further, they were carefully scrutinized and quickly dismissed for evidences of immoral behavior -- and morality itself was judged narrowly by today's standards. Home, school, and religious institutions were joined in character development and the general upbringing of children and youth.

From the perspective of distance, one of the most significant changes to take place within the educational system over the past four to five decades is bureaucratization. There was no superintendent and no central staff in the district where I went to school; nor did such exist in the larger district where I later taught. In the latter, the board hired (largely on the basis of an interview, with many candidates for each position) and fired (largely on the basis of an annual report on each teacher by the provincial school inspector). The secretary of the board (not an educator usually), commonly employed only part-time, saw to it that the few textbooks and essential materials were parcelled out to each school in a roughly equitable way. Principals taught and, therefore, were "inspected" as teachers; their administrative abilities included "discipline" and were judged largely on hearsay. Each school was, virtually by the facts of circumstances, a tub on its own bottom.

This last is what has been most lost over the intervening years of growth and almost inevitable bureaucratization. Space limitations force me to leap over this part of our recent educational history. Instead, I invoke once again the metaphor -- apples, diamonds, and glue -- as it comes up on my mental television screen when I contemplate the parallel history of educational reform efforts.

Increasing refinement and use of the conventional linear model of change has accompanied virtually all areas of bureaucratization in modern life. Neither this model nor bureaucracy is by definition bad. Both have their legitimate uses. However, when the former is adopted by the latter as THE way to get changes effected quickly and efficiently where more of the workers work, and when those at the top of the bureaucratic pyramid, far removed from where the workers work, make more and more decisions FOR those who are to carry them out, dissonance usually sets in. This is so even where the relationship between inputs and outputs is rather easily determined. When these relationships are vague, at best, the process can by dysfunctional. This is strikingly the case in education and schooling.

Examination of successive reform eras in schooling over decades reveals parallels. The rhetoric of problem or need is almost invariably global. It is schools and schooling that need fixing. "If an unfriendly foreign power had attempted to impose on America the mediocre educational performance that exists today," wrote the National Commission on Excellence in Education in A Nation at Risk (1983, P. 5), "we might well have viewed it as an act of war." In 1957, following the launching of Sputnik, our schools were associated with declining ability of this nation to compete technologically with the U.S.S.R. But the proposed remedies, in 1957 and today, invariably have been piecemeal and the same in both eras: more math, more science, more homework, more time in school, tougher standards for students, brighter teachers, academic majors for teachers, tests for teachers, etc. Thrust into schools, the implied assortment of interventions will make things right; schools will become excellent again. We have heard these things before. Had they worked following Sputnik, surely there would be no need to invoke them again. Our schools would have become and remained good, perhaps even excellent.

What the improvement effort did then and what it is doing now is to spawn the most extraordinary assortment of reform goodies, for the most part attractively packaged, and an equally extraordinary array of entrepreneurs -- salespeople, hucksters, and even some artful dodgers -- to market them. A superintendent, principal, teacher, accountant just

49

yesterday; an educational consultant today. Have business cards, will travel. One has only to "visit the booths" at a major educational conference to appreciate and be simultaneously bewildered by this awesome arsenal and its human entourage.

Dare one, should one, criticize all of this? Not I, for one. And it would make not one whit of difference were I to. Indeed, mindlessly cruising the booths recently, I encountered myself cloned and seemingly "live on television," in an authorized video tape series on school renewal. Next door, I found myself in print, quoted extensively (unauthorized, I think), ostensibly for the purpose of giving implicit credence to a package neither known to or understood by me. Various items in this melange will be carried with varying degrees of success by couriers, much as Salesman Sam carried apples, diamonds, and glue to the assorted barrels of the storekeepers in his territory.

But what was significantly different about Sam is that he carried his goods directly to a purchaser who knew his clients and whose personal future depended on how well he knew and served them. Undoubtedly, there was a lot of empty space in the barrel labelled "diamonds."

But most of the purchasing of educational consultants and assorted packaged wares is by people far removed from those who are to use them and, presumably, profit from this use. Further, both their use and the kind of profit that is to occur often are mandated. Get your reading scores up and use this method and this package to do it. And you will be held accountable for the results.

Meanwhile, over in other arenas of educational reform is much talk of teaching as a profession and higher salaries for professional teachers. Who are then to be told what methods and packages to use? Come now. What kind of expectation is this for professionals?

Teachers, individually and in groups, increasingly are becoming aware of the contradictions inherent in this doublespeak. In various parts of the country, not necessarily questioning the potential usefulness of goodies foisted on them, teachers are questioning both the wisdom of others imposing on them how they should teach and with what and the right of these "others" to do so. They are challenging the honesty of being told that there is no money for site-based staff development and school renewal, when someone in the district office is requiring their participation in a consultant-led workshop on teaching.

They are gristling, too, at deepening their knowledge of their subjects, learning alternative ways to teach and earning master's degrees -- as professionals should -- on their own time and money only to be required to follow district mandates, whether or not in keeping with their professional knowledge.

There is another model of change which is at least as viable and useful as the more commonly understood and used linear one. It, too, has a long and respectable lineage under a variety of labels and is showing up in the literature today quite frequently under the rubric "ecological." It views the educational system as an ecosystem becoming increasingly healthy (not healthful) as the school (an open system or culture) is supported at the center of a larger, supportive infrastructure. Instead of elements in this infrastructure ordering up apples, diamonds, and glue for a passively receptive school, teachers at the school site, exercising the authority granted to them and assuming the responsibility of professionals, decide that they need bread, honey, and milk.

Why do we tippy-toe around such a scenario? Oh yes, it's there in our rhetoric. But, at the level of potential action, we make excuses. Each school will be so different (exactly what many parents who ultimately choose private schools look to find for their children). Many principals are not able to provide the necessary leadership. True, but much of what they need to know is known. Why not provide the conditions they need for this learning -- and then let them return with dignity to the classroom if they are not providing the necessary leadership within two to three years? Teachers won't or can't learn to assume the necessary responsibility. Let's just drop this piece of garbage into the disposal where it belongs.

Once upon a time, principals and teachers, with each school tub on its own bottom, assumed this responsibility very well, and were respected and trusted to boot. But that was before we learned so much about what teachers should do and commandeered so many people, in and out of education, to tell them how to do it. Are we, perhaps, overlooking the main reason for approaching site-based, teacher-driven school renewal so gingerly? Is it possible that many of us are well-served by the way things are and would like to keep them that way?

I don't think I would go back to Salesman Sam, in the comic strip or real life, even if I could. But I can't. I've seen enough good schools in my time to know that the best thing about the three schools I attended was that I was young. I know, too, that there is available now a veritable treasure chest of educational apples, diamonds, glue, and more for teachers to use and a large stable of people eager and willing to help teachers work with children in ways my teachers at best could only have imagined.

What a shame that so much of this bountiful resource is going to waste because of misuse. We havo loarned a lot about how to keep school better. What we have lost sight of, while learning so much about education and teaching, is that adults learn, more or less, as children do. That is, they learn most easily what they see use for. "Use" is in the eyes of the beholder. It can be as abstract (for some of us) as enlarging on a store of memorized poetry. Or use can be as concrete as securing a loose board with a nail.

Of course, we rarely seek to learn what we do not know exists. And so, the infrastructure supporting teachers renewing their schools must do more than deliver apples, diamonds, and glue when requested. It puts these and more in barrels where they are visible to tease and perhaps titillate until sought out. Those of us who have learned so much, including what is best for all of us, are surprised to learn that apples give some of us indigestion, that some of us consider diamonds to be ostentatious, and that some of us use glue for purposes not intended.

SELECTED BIBLIOGRAPHY

BOOKS:

The Elementary School. Englewood Cliffs, New Jersey: Prentice-Hall, Inc., 1956. Pp. 474. (with Herrick, Estvan, and Eberman). Translated into Spanish. (Enoch Pratt Library Committee Selection as one of the best education books for 1956).

Educational Leadership and the Elementary School Principal. New York: Holt, Rinehart, and Winston, 1956. Pp. 371. (With Spain and Drummond).

The Nongraded Elementary School. Rev. ed. New York: Harcourt Brace Jovanovich, Inc., 1963. Pp. 248. (With Robert H. Anderson). Translated into Japanese, Spanish, Italian & Hebrew. (1st ed., 1959, Enoch Pratt Library Committee Selector as one of the best education books for 1959).

Planning and Organizing for Teaching. Washington: National Education Association, 1963. Pp. 190.

The Changing American School, Editor. Sixty-fifth Yearbook of the National Society for the Study of Education, Part II. Chicago: The University of Chicago Press, 1966. Pp. 319.

Computers and Information Systems in Education. New York: Harcourt Brace Jovanovich, Inc., 1966. Pp. 152. (With O'Toole and Tyler).

School, Curriculum, and the Individual. Waltham, Massachusetts: Xerox College Publishing Company, 1966. Pp. 259. Translated into Spanish.

The Changing School Curriculum. New York: Fund for the Advancement of Education, 1966. Pp. 122.

Behind the Classroom Door. Worthington, Ohio: Charles A. Jones Publishing Company, 1970. Pp. 120. (With Klein and Associates). (Pi Lambda Theta selection for one of the best education books for 1970-71); Translated into Hebrew; Revised and retitled, Looking Behind the Classroom Door, 1974. Pp. 152.

The Elementary School in the United States, Co-editor. The Seventy-second Yearbook of the National Society for the Study of Education, Part II. Chicago: The University of Chicago Press, 1973. Pp. 418. (Identified as one of the outstanding books in education for 1972-73 by Pi Lambda Theta).

Early Schooling in the United States. New York: McGraw-Hill Book Company, 1973. Pp. 240. (With Klein, Novotney and Associates).

Early Schooling in England and Israel. New York: McGraw-Hill Gook Company, 1973. Pp. 127. (With Feshbach and Lombard).

Toward A Mankind School: An Adventure in Humanistic Education. New York: McGraw-Hill Book Company, 1974. Pp. 193. (With Klein, Novotney, Tye and Associates). Translated into Japanese.

The Conventional and the Alternative in Education. Berkeley: McCutchan Publishing Corporation, 1975. Pp. 276. (With others).

The Dynamics of Educational Change: Toward Responsive Schools. New York: McGraw-Hill Book Company, 1975. Pp. 267.

Facing the Future: Issues in Education and Schooling. New York: McGraw-Hill Book Company, 1976. Pp. 274.

Curriculum Inquiry: The Study of Curriculum Practice. New York: McGraw-Hill Book Company, 1979. Pp. 371. (With others).

What Schools Are For. Bloomington, Indiana: Phi Delta Kappa Educational Foundation, 1979. Pp. 128. Excerpt entitled "What Schools Should Be For," in Learning, 9, No. 1 (July-August, 1980), 38-43.

Individual Differences and the Common Curriculum, Co-editor. The Eighty-second Yearbook of the National Society for the Study of Education, Part I. Chicago: The University of Chicago Press, 1983. Pp. 339.

A Place Called School: Prospects for the Future. New York: McGraw-Hill Book Company, 1984. Pp. 396. (Received the First Distinguished Book-of-the-year Award from Kappa Delta Pi; received the American Educational Research Association 1985 Outstanding Book Award).

ARTICLES IN JOURNALS, ENCYCLOPEDIAS, ETC:

"A Typology of Educational Alternatives," Alternatives in Education, No. 4 in New Directions for Education (Winter, 1973), 1-25.

"Studying and Effecting Educational Change," UCLA Educator, 17 (Fall, 1974), 5-8.

"An Emphasis on Change," American Education, 11 (January-February, 1975), 16-21, 24-25, 28.

"A Perspective on Accountability," Phi Delta Kappan, 57, No. 2 (October, 1975), 108-12.

"Schools Can Make a Difference," Educational Leadership, 33, No. 2 (November, 1975), 108-17.

"Developing Comprehensive Educational Systems and Programs," Bulletin (Victorian Institute of Educational Research, Melbourne, Australia), 35 (November, 1975), 31-45.

"A Strategy for Improving School Arts Programs," The Journal of Aesthetic Education, 10 (July-October, 1976), 151-63.

"Alternative Schooling: Language and Meaning," Today's Education, 66, No. 1 (January-February, 1977), 84-86.

"An Array of Educative Agencies," (response to William C. Norris, "Via Technology to a New Era in Education,") Phi Delta Kappan, 58, No. 6 (February, 1977), 454-55.

"What Goes On In Our Schools?," Educational Researcher, 6 No. 3 (March, 197), 3-6.

"An Ecological Approach to Change in Elementary School Settings," The Elementary School Journal, 78, No. 2 (November, 1977), 95-105. A slightly different version of this paper appears in Baylor Educator (Spring, 1976), 3-14, and in Facing the Future: Issues in Education and Schooling (McGraw-Hill, 1976), 167-86.

"Educational Leadership: Toward the Third Era," Educational Leadership, 35, No. 4 (January, 1978), 322-24, 326-27, 329-31. Abstract of this paper appears under title, "First Things at the Center," Thrust (--For Educational Leadership), 7, No. 3 (January, 1978), 3-4.

"The Trouble With Humanistic Education," Journal of Humanistic Education (January/February, 1978), 8-30.

"On the Cultivation and Corruption of Education," The Educational Forum, XLII (March, 1978), 267-78.

"What Schools Are For: An American Perspective on the Green Paper," Trends in Education, 1 (Spring Issue, 1978), 40-49. (London: Her Majesty's Stationery Office).

"Can Our Schools Get Better?," Phi Delta Kappan, 60, No. 5 (January, 1979), 342-47. (Abstract published in Pennsylvania Schoolmaster, 10, No. 2 (April, 1978), 10-11, 16).

"Schooling: Issues and Answers," St Louis Post-Dispatch, Centennial Edition, March 25, 1979, sec. "Ideals in Transition: Tomorrow's America," 70-73.

"An Overview of 'A Study of Schooling'," Phi Delta Kappan, 61, No. 3 (November, 1979), 174-78.

"Are School Boards Strong Enough to Champion the Best Interests of Students?." Updating School Board Policies, 11, No. 1 (January, 1980), 1-3, 6.

"A Letter to Secretary Hufstedler," The Networker, 1, No. 2 (Winter, 1980), 3.

"How Laboratory Schools Go Awry," UCLA Educator, 21, No. 2 (Winter, 1980), 47-53.

"How Fares the Common School?," Today's Education, 69, No. 2 (April-May, 1980), 37-40.

"What We Don't Know About Schooling," Phi Delta Kappan, 61, No. 9 (May, 1980), 591-92.

"Networking and Educational Improvement: Reflections on a Strategy." Paper commissioned by National Institute of Education (DHEW), Washington, D. C., School Capacity for Problem Solving Group, Network Development Division, March, 1977. Reproduced by ERIC Document Reproduction Service, ED 180 433, dated May 7, 1980.

"What Should Schools Do?," California School Boards, 39, No. 6 (September, 1980), 11-16.

"Perspective/The Dean: The State of the School," Network (UCLA Graduate School of Education News) 1, No. 1 (September, 1980), 1, 14-15.

"Perspective/The Dean," Network (UCLA Graduate School of Education News) 1, No. 3 (April, 1981), 3.

"Perspective/The Dean: 1981 State-of-the-School Address," Network (UCLA Graduate School of Education News) 1, No. 4 (July, 1981), 3-6.

"Perspective/The Dean: 1981 Convocation Address," Network (UCLA Graduate School of Education News) 2, No. 1 (September, 1981), 5-6.

"Curriculum Development Beyond 1980," Educational Evaluation and Policy Analysis, 3, No. 5 (September-October,1981),49-54.

"John Goodlad and Marilyn Kourilsky Address Board of UCLA Foundation," Network (UCLA Graduate School of Education News) 2, No. 2 (December, 1981), 6-9.

"An Agenda For Improving Our Schools," The Executive Review, 2, No. 8 (May, 1982). PP. 6.

"Let's Get on With the Reconstruction," Phi Delta Kappan, 64, No. 1 (September, 1982), 19-20.

"What is Worth Knowing?," Alumnus (Southern Illinois University at Edwardsville), 10, No. 4 (Fall, 1982), 2-5. Also printed under title, "Commencement Address," Seedbed (Southern Illinois University at Edwardsville, Teachers' Center Project) 12 (August, 1982), 66-75.

"The Quality of Education in Schools," The Iowa Curriculum Bulletin, 7, No. 1 (Fall, 1982), 42-45.

"A Study of Schooling: Some Findings and Hypotheses," Phi Delta Kappan, 64, No. 7 (March, 1983), 465-70.

"Improving Schooling in the 1980s: Toward the Non-Replication of Non-Events," Educational Leadership, 40, No. 7 (April, 1983), 4-7.

"What Some Schools and Classrooms Teach," Educational Leadership, 40, No. 7 (April, 1983), 8-19.

"A Study of Schooling: Some Implications for School Improvement," Phi Delta Kappan, 64, No. 8 (April, 1983), 552-58.

"John Goodlad Responds: On Dogma and Straw Men," Educational Leadership, 40, No. 8 (May, 1983), 53-55.

"Teaching: An Endangered Profession," Teachers College Record, 84, No. 3, (Spring, 1983), 575-78.

"Access To Knowledge," Teachers College Record, 84, No. 4, (Summer, 1983), 787-800.

"Understanding Schools is Basic to Improving Them," The Canadian School Executive, 3, No. 9 (March, 1984), 3-10.

"Introduction: The Uncommon Common School," Education and Urban Society: The Common School in a Multicultural Society (edited by author and Thomas David) 16, No. 3 (May, 1984), 243-52.

"Curriculum as a Field of Study," <u>International Encyclopedia of Education</u>, (edited by Torsten Husen and T. Neville Postlethwaite), 1985, 1141-44.

"The Great American Schooling Experiment," <u>Phi Delta Kappan</u>, 67, No. 4 (December, 1985), 266-71.

"Toward A More Perfect Union," <u>State Education Leader</u>, 5 No. 2 (Spring, 1986), 1, 8-9.

"School-University Collaboration: Is a Symbiotic Relationship Feasible?," <u>Wingspan</u>, 2, No. 2 (June, 1986), 3-10.

"The Learner at the World's Center," <u>Social Education</u> (October, 1986), 424-36.

Alice Sterling Honig

AUTOBIOGRAPHICAL SKETCH OF ALICE STERLING HONIG

<u>Current Position</u>: Professor of Child Development, College for Human Development, Syracuse University

<u>Area(s) of Expertise</u>: Infancy, childcare, parenting, iron deficiency, infant/toddler assessment, language interactions, prosocial development

<u>Mentor</u>: Dr. Bettye M. Caldwell

<u>Background Experiences</u>:
Program Director of the Family Development Research Program and Children's Center (1965-77)

Research Review Editor for <u>Young Children</u>

North American Editor for <u>Early Child Development and Care</u>

Cross-cultural research in Bilan de Sante Clinic, Paris, France

Director of the National Annual Quality Infant/Toddler Caregiving Workshops at Syracuse University for past eleven years

Member of Board of Directors of Nurturing World Child Care Center

Member of Board of Directors of Resources for Child Care Management, Inc.

CARING AND KINDNESS: CURRICULAR GOALS FOR EARLY CHILDHOOD EDUCATORS

Cognitive enrichment has been the main concern of innovative early childhood education (ECE) programs for decades. Without such enrichment, disadvantaged youngsters showed a typical downward drift of IQ from infancy onward and often difficulties with early learning in the elementary school. Pioneer ECE programs demonstrated their efficacy by showing how IQ downward spirals were prevented. For example, the Milwaukee program served infants, toddlers and preschoolers whose mothers lived in dilapidated housing, had few or no job skills and IQs under 80. By five years of age, children who had attended this intensive enrichment program attained mean IQs of 124, compared to the mean of 90 attained by control peers (Hever & Garber, 1975.)

Typically, during school years, program children showed erosion of initial IQ gains over time. Frequently, supports for early learning were not maintained at home nor were they individually possible in large elementary school classes. Control youngsters entering school began to score higher, and differences between them and experimental children disappeared in the early grades.

However, even more disturbing social data became available from longitudinal studies. Kindergarten children, graduates of the North Carolina Abecedarian project, were observed to carry out 15 times as many aggressive actions toward peers on the playground as disadvantaged controls who had not attended the high quality ECE program. Also, teachers rated program children in class, hallway, and lunchroom as more aggressive than their peers (Haskins, 1985). What had happened?

In their concern and efforts to break the downward IQ spiral, ECE models had not concentrated on the equally necessary positive social skills children need to succeed in encounters with peers and teachers. After a program entitled "My Friends and Me" was implemented with a later group of Abecedarian children, higher rates of aggressive behaviors were no longer observed in playground peer interactions.

Implementing a prosocial curriculum is a crucial and important goal for early childhood education programs. Antisocial children are

60

deflected from learning as they engage in inappropriate and hurtful interactions. The motivational roots of learning must be considered as well as congitive skills.

Programs that have emphasized classroom cooperation and altruism do report more hopeful outcomes in the social domain. More mature levels of conflict resolution and negotiation strategies, while playing a board game, were found for preschoolers enrolled in a Constructivist classroom in comparison with peers attending a Montessori program (Devries & Goncu, in press). The Perry Preschool Project emphasized social skills and active child participation in construction of knowledge. Young adults who had attended this program 19 years earlier were involved in significantly fewer delinquent acts compared to controls (Berrueta-Clement et al., 1984).

The Family Development Research Program (FDRP) (Lally & Honig, 1977), an omnibus child care and home visitation program, strongly supported a more intense, loving relationship between parents and children and sustained Eriksonian trust building between caregivers and the infants in their charge (Honig, 1987). Children were encouraged to generate prosocial rather than aggressive solutions to their problems with peers. Fifteen years later, FDRP teenagers had committed far fewer delinquencies, and much less serious ones, than control children not in the program (Lally et al., 1987).

These data support the importance of a more enlightened conceptualization of ECE programs. Prosocial goals must be specifically included and actively implemented if children are to learn to become more altruistic, helpful, and caring. Kindness belongs in the ECE curriculum. It is hard work for young children to learn to decenter (to take the point of view of others), to empathize with others' hurts, to share, and to cooperate.

Researchers provide helpful hints that can be translated into curricular ideas to enhance the caring quality of classrooms and homes. What have we learned from researchers?

1. Mothers who hold infants tenderly, feed them sensitively, and respond promptly and contingently to distress have more securely attached, more cooperative toddlers (Ainsworth, 1982).

2. Secure, loving attachment of infant to parent leads to later toddler cooperation and compliance with parent suggestions for solving

difficult tool-using tasks (Sroufe, 1979).

3.   Teachers who are nurturant, structure real life situations for preschoolers to be helpful, and also use dioramas and pictures to engage children in dialogues about how to be helpful and kind, enhance child altruism (Yarrow, Scott, & Waxler, 1973).

4.   Parents in low-income families who show genuine interest in their children, read to them, talk lots at dinner and are proud of their children's helpfulness with chores, have children with a sense of humor, who get along well with teachers and peers, and are well-motivated learners (Swan & Stavos, 1973).

5.   When teachers preached charitableness but were stingy and did not donate for poor children, then children donated few of their own game winnings (Bryan & Walbek, 1970). Modeling altruism is vital. Caregivers need to practice what they preach.

6.   Children who watched more violent TV shows at age eight were significantly more likely at age 19 to have arrest records, motor vehicle violations, and peer nominations as aggresive persons (Eron, 1987).

7.   Children who, for one month, watched Mr. Rogers Neighborhood, a TV program emphasizing friendliness and helpfulness, showed increased ability to delay gratification and behave more prosocially with peers (Friedrich & Stein, 1973).

8.   Mothers of girls and fathers of boys who were nominated as most likely to be considerate and helpful by their fifth-grade classmates ranked altruism high in their own hierarchy of values (Hoffman, 1975). Children, whose mothers responded in a tender, concerned manner, remained more altruistic in follow-up studies five years later (Pines, 1979). "Nurturant parents provide models of prosocial behaviors for their children" (Honig, 1982, p. 56).

9.   Parents, after divorce, who remained loving and involved on a consistent basis with their children had the most well-adjusted, least oppositional, or regressing children several years later (Wallerstein & Kelly, 1980).

10. Parents who used an authoritative style (reflecting unconditional commitment to the child, high expectations, firm rules and

reasoning, and interested engagement) rather than a permissive or authoritarian style had the most cooperative children at home and at school (Baumrind, 1977).

11. When mainstreaming school emphasized prosocial development, typical and atypical peers were equally likely to be prosocial toward their own or the other group. But atypical peers had much lower rates of prosocial interaction. Mainstreaming per se does not enhance prosocial interactions. Teachers must plan for, model, and provide experiences (such as icing a cake together) that galvanize and promote prosocial interactions (Honig & McCarron, in press).

12. Teachers who used ego boosting rather than ordering or criticizing in response to toddler behaviors received much higher rates of compliance (Honig & Wittmer, 1982).

13. Teachers who taught children to understand "same" and "different" feelings, to think about the consequences of their social behaviors, and to generate as many alternative solutions as possible to solve their interpersonal conflicts, reported less aggression and less withdrawn behavior in early elementary school children (Shure & Spivack, 1978).

14. Moral internalization and resistance to temptation was higher in children whose parents used reasoning and explanations (inductive discipline) more frequently (Hoffman, 1975).

Conclusions

These research findings can stimulate creativity in program planners, directors, and teachers to devise and implement classroom techniques and parent involvement efforts in order to promote prosocial behaviors. In addition, bibliotherapy materials make an excellent teaching tool. Many books for children provide good models of how children, adults, and animals act helpful, protective, kind, generous, thoughtful, and loyal with others. Horton Hatches an Egg and Horton Hears a Who, by Dr. Seuss, are two fine examples of such picture books.

The caring classroom must be nurtured by vigorous applications of teacher responsive attunement, empathy, explanations, shared dialogue, role modeling of kindness and courtesy, praise and encouragement for prosocial actions, and ingenuity. Then early

Childhood educators will be able to boast of raising their children's CQ, Caring Quotient, as today they emphasize raising children's IQ.

References

Ainsworth, M. D. (1982). Early caregiving and later patterns of attachment. In M. H. Klaus & M. O. Robertson (Eds.), Birth, interaction and attachment. Skillman, NJ: Johnson & Johnson.

Baumrind, D. (1977). Some thoughts about childrearing. In S. Cohen & T. J. Comiskey (Eds.), Child development: Contemporary perspectives. Itasca, IL: Peacock.

Berrueta-Clement, J. R., Schweinhart, L. J., Barnett, W. S., Epstein, A. S., & Weikart, D. P. (1984). Changed lives: The effects of the Perry preschool program on youths through age 19. (Monographs of the High/Scope Educational Research Foundation, 8). Ypsilanti, MI: High/Scope Press.

Bryan, J. H. & Walbek, N. (1970). The impact of words and deeds concerning altruism upon children. Child Development, 41, 747-759.

Devries, R. & Goncu, A. (in press). Interpersonal relations in four-year-old dyads from Constuctivist and Montessori Programs. In A. S. Honig (Ed.), Optimizing early child care and education (Special Issue). Early Child Development and Care, 30.

Eron, L. D. (1987). The development of aggressive behavior from the perspective of a developing behaviorism. American Psychologist, 42(5), 435-442.

Friedrich, L. K. & Stein, A. H. (1973). Aggressive and prosocial television programs and the natural behavior of preschool children. Monographs of the Society for Research in Child Development, 38 (4).

Hasking, R. (1985). Public school aggression among children with varying day care experiences. Child Development, 56, 689-703.

Heber, R. & Garber, H. (1975). The Milwaukee Project: A study of the use of family intervention to prevent cultural-familial retardation. In B. Z. Friedlander, B. M. Sterritt, & G. E. Kirk (Eds.), Exceptional infant. Vol. 3. Assessment and Intervention. New York: Brunner/Mazel.

Hoffman, M. L. (1975). Altruistic behavior and the parent-child relationship. Journal of personality and social psychology, 31, 937-943.

Honig, A. S. (1982). Research in review: Prosocial development in children. Young Children, 37(5), 51-62.

Honig, A. S. (1987). The Eriksonian approach: Infant-toddler education. In J. Roopnarine & J. Johnson (Eds.), Approaches to early childhood education (pp. 49-69). Columbus, OH: Charles E. Merrill.

Honig, A. S. & McCarron, P. (in press). Prosocial behaviors of handicapped and typical peers in an integrated preschool. In A. S. Honig, (Ed.), Optimizing early child care and education (Special Issue). Early Child Development and Care, 30.

Honig, A. S. & Wittmer, D. S. (1982). Teachers and low-income toddlers in metropolitan day care. Early Child Development and Care, 10, 95-112.

Lally, J. R. & Honig, A. S. (1977). The Family Development Research Program: A program for prenatal, infant and early childhood enrichment. In M. Day & R. Parker (Eds.), The preschool in action (2nd ed.). Boston, MA: Allyn & Bacon.

Lally, J. R., Mangione, P., Honig, A. S., & Hans, S. (1987, March). The Family Development Research Program: History of the Project. Paper presented at the biennial meeting of the Society for Research in Child Development, Baltimore, MD.

Pines, M. (1979). Good samaritans at age two? Psychology Today, 13(1), 66-77.

Shure, M. B. & Spivack, G. (1978). Problem-solving techniques in childrearing. San Francisco, CA: Jossey-Bass.

Sroufe, L.A. (1979). The coherence of individual development: Early care, attachment, and subsequent developmental issues. American Psychologist, 34, 834-841.

Swan, R. W. & Stavros, H. (1973). Child rearing practices associated with the development of cognitive skills of children in low socioeconomic areas. Early Child Development and Care, 2, 23-38.

Wallerstein, J. S. & Kelly, J. K. (1980). Surviving the breakup: How children cope with divorce. New York: Basic Books.

Yarrow, M. R., Scott, P. M., & Waxler, C. Z. (1973). Learning concern for others. Developmental Psychology, 8, 240-260.

SELECTED BIBLIOGRAPHY

PUBLICATIONS & REPORTS:

Honig, A. S. (1985). Ask Dr. Honig. Caring for infants and Toddlers, 1(1), 14-15.

Honig, A. S. (1985). Discipline tips for teachers. New York Early Education Reporter, 31(2), 4-5.

Honig, A. S. (1985). High quality infant/toddler care: Issues and dilemmas. Young Children, 41(1), 40-46. [ERIC Document Reproduction Service No. ED 255 322]

Honig, A. S. (1985). Love and learn: Discipline for Young Children. Washington, D.C. National Association for the Education of Young Children.

Honig, A. S. (1985). Research in review: Compliance, control and discipline (Part I). Young Children, 40(2), 50-58.

Honig, A. S. (1985). Research in review: Compliance, control and discipline (Part II). Young Children, 40(3), 47-52.

Honig, A. S. (1985). [Review of Family life and school achievement: Why poor black children succeed or fail]. Young Children, 40(4), p. 60.

Honig, A. S. (1985). [Review of J. R. Berrueta-Clement, L. J. Schweinhart, W. S. Barnett, A. S. Epstein, & D. P. Weikart, Changed lives: The effects of the Perry preschool program on youths through age 19.] Young Children, 40(5), p. 58.

Honig, A. S. (1985). [Review of S. Gordon & J. Gordon, A better safe than sorry book: A family guide for sexual assault prevention.] Young Children, 41(1), pp. 60-61.

Honig, A. S. (1985). Sexual assault prevention [Review of S. Gordon & J. Gordon, A better safe than sorry book: A family guide for sexual assault prevention]. Day Care and Early Education, 12(3), p. 43.

Honig, A. S. (1985). The art of talking to a baby. Working Mother, 8(3), 72-78.

Honig, A. S. (1985). Understanding children's behavior in groups. Syracuse, NY: Syracuse University College for Human Development. [ERIC Document Reproduction No. PS015222]

Honig, A. S. & Gardner, C. (1985). Overwhelmed mothers of toddlers in immigrant families: Stress factors. In Abstracts of the biennial meeting of the Society for Research in Child Development, Volume 5. Chicago: University of Chicago, p. 57. [ERIC Document No. ED 254 347]

Honig, A. S., Gardner, C., & Vesin, C. (1985). Stress factors among overwhelmed mothers of toddlers in North African immigrant families in Paris. Caiers de psychologie cognitive, 5 (No. 3/4), 277-278.

66

Honig, A. S. & Wittmer, D. S. (1985). Early signs of sex role stereotyping among day care toddlers. Syracuse, NY: Syracuse University, College for Human Development. [ERIC Document Reproduction Service No. PS014801]

Honig, A. S. & Wittmer, D. S. (1985). Toddler bids and teacher responses. Child Care Quarterly, 14(1), 14-29.

Roopnarine, J. L. & Honig, A. S. (1985). Research in review. The unpopular child. Young Children, 40(6), 59-64.

Wittmer, D. S. & Honig, A. S. (1985). Child effects on teacher behavior. In Abstracts of the biennial meeting of the Society for Research in Child Development, Volume 5, Chicago: University of Chicago Press, p. 370.

Honig, A. S. (1986, Winter). Ask Dr. Honig. Caring for infants and toddlers, 1(2), 15.

Honig, A. S. (1986, Spring). Ask Dr. Honig. Caring for infants and toddlers, 1(4), 14.

Honig, A. S. (1986, Summer). Education is key to parenting perplexities. The Art of Parenting, 6(3), 1.

Honig, A. S. (1986). Emerging issues in early childhood education (Part 1). Day Care and Early Education, 13(3), 6-11.

Honig, A. S. (1986). Emerging issues in early childhood education (Part 2). Day Care and early Education, 13(4), 22-27.

Honig, A. S. (1986). Emerging issues in early childhood education (Part 3). Day Care and Early Education, 14(1), 20-23.

Honig, A. S. (1986). Helpful hints for parents in choosing child care. [Review of J. Miller & S. Weissman, The Parents' Guide to Day Care.] Young Children, 41(6), 73.

Honig, A. S. (Ed.) (1986). Risk factors in infancy. London, England: Gordon & Breach Science Publishers.

Honig, A. S. (1986). Research in review: Stress and coping in children, (Part 1), Young Children, 41(4), 50-63.

Honig, A. S. (1986). Research in review: Stress and coping in children, (Part 2), Young Children, 41(5), 47-59.

Honig, A. S. (1986). Tuning into toddlers: A communication challenge. Early Child Development and Care, 25, 207-219.

Wittmer, D. S. & Honig, A. S. (1986). Indicators of well-being and distress. Caring for Infants and Toddlers, 1(2), 3-6.

Honig A. S., Caldwell, B. M., & Richmond, J. B. (1986). Infancy intervention: Historical perspectives. Early Child Development and Care, 26, 89-93.

Honig, A. S. & McCarron, P. A. (1986). Prosocial behaviors between handicapped and nonhandicapped peers in an integrated preschool. New apporaches to infant, child, adolescent, and family mental health: Abstracts (p. 594). Paris, France: International Association for Child and Adolescent Psychiatry and Allied Professions (11th International Congress).

Wittmer, D. S. & Honig, A. S. (1986). Teacher re-creation of negative interactions with toddlers. Abstracts of the Third World Congress on Infant Psychiatry and Allied Disciplines (p. 117). Stockholm, Sweden.

Honig, A. S. & Wittmer, D. S. (1986). Teacher-toddler day care interactions: Where, what, how. In D. Tamir, A.Russell, & T. B. Brazelton (Eds.), Intervention and stimulation in infant development (pp. 165-174). London: Freund Publishers.

Honig, A. S. (1987). Development of academically competent children. Early Childhood Update, 3(1), 2-3.

Honig, A. S. (1987). Infant attachment: key to competence and cooperation? [In I. Bretherton & E. Waters (Eds.), Growing points of attachment theory and research. Monographs of the Society for Research in Child Development, 50 (1-2, Serial No. 209)]. Contemporary Psychology.

Honig, A. S. (1987). Early parenting and later child achievement. In A. S. Honig (Ed.), Early parenting and later child achievement (Special issue). Early Child Development and Care, 27(2), 215-228.

Honig, A. S. (Ed.), (1987). Early parenting and later child achievement (Special issue). Early Child Development and Care, 27(2).

Honig, A. S. (1987). [In E. F. Griffin, Island of Childhood: Education in the special world of nursery school. New York: Teachers College Press]. Young Children, 42(2), 88-89.

Honig, A. S. (1987). The Eriksonian approach: Infant-toddler education. In J. Roopnarine & J. Johnson (Eds.) Approaches to early childhood education (pp. 49-69). Columbus, OH: Charles E. Merrill.

Honig, A. S. (1987, January). How to spot top-notch day care. Working Mother, 10(1), 72-73.

Honig, A. S. (1987). Preface. In L. Schrag & A. Godwin (Eds.), Setting up for infant care: Guidelines for centers and family day care. Washington, DC: National Association for the Education of Young Children.

Honig, A. S. (1987). Research in review: The shy child. Young Children, 42(1), 54-64.

Honig, A. S., Gardner, K., & Vesin, C. (1987). Stress factors among overwhelmed mothers of toddlers in North African immigrant families. Early Child Development and Care, 28(2), 37-46.

Honig, A. S. & Wittmer, D. S. (1987). Caregiver interaction and sex of toddler. Journal of Research in Childhood Education.

Honig, A. S., Wittmer, D. S. & Gibralter, J. (1987). Discipline, cooperation and compliance: An annotated bibliography, Catalog#. Urbana, IL: ERIC Clearinghouse on Elementary and Early Childhood Education.

Lally, J. R., Mangione, P., Honig, A. S. & Hans, S. (1987, March). The Family Development Research Program: History of the project. Abstracts of the Biennial Meeting of the Society for Research in Child Development, Vol. 6, pp. 373-374.

Wittmer, D. S. & Honig, A. S. (1987). Do boy toddlers bug teachers more? Canadian Children, 12(1), 21-27.

Honig, A. S. (1988). Assessing the preparation of infant/toddler caregivers. In S. Kilmer (Ed.) Advances in Early Education and Day Care, Vol. 5. Greenwich, CT, JAI Press.

Honig, A. S. (1988). Caring and kindness: Curricular goals for early childhood educators. In G. F. Roberson & M. Johnson (Eds), Educational leaders: Their views of contemporary issues. Lanham, MD: University Press of America.

Honig, A. S. (1988). The Family Development Research Program: History of the Project. In D. Powell (Ed.).

Honig, A. S. (1988). Infant-toddler caregiving: Are there magic recipes? In R. Lurie & R. Neugebauer (Eds.), Infant/toddler caregiving: What works, what doesn't, Vol. 3. Richmond, WA: Child Care Information Exchange.

Honig, A. S. (1988). Kindergarten for young fives - yes or no? Scripps-Howard Newspapers.

Honig, A. S. (1988). Research: A tool to promote optimal early child care and education. In A. S. Honig (Ed.), Optimizing early child care and education (Special issue). Early Child Development and Care, 30.

Honig, A. S. (1988). Your child's emotional development. In A. Fischoff (Ed.), Readings for family volunteers. Eugene, OR: Birth to three Program.

Honig, A. S. & Lally, J. R. (1988). Behavior profiles of experienced teachers of infants. In A. S. Honig (Ed.), Optimizing early child care and education (Special issue). Early Child Development and Care, 30.

Honig, A. S. & Lally, J. R. (1988). Effects of testing style on language scores of four-year-old low-income "control" children. Submitted for publication.

Honig, A. S. & McCarron, P. A. (1988, April). Prosocial behaviors of handicapped and typical peers in an integrated preschool. In A. S. Honig, (Ed.), Optimizing early child care and education (Special Issue). Early Child Development and Care, 30.

Honig, A. S. & Wittmer, D. S. (1988). Socialization and discipline. In J. R. Lally (Ed.).

Jerome, M. A., Honig, A. S., & Coplan, J. (1988). Validation of the early language milestone scale in a low risk population. Submitted for publication.

Wittmer, D. S. & Honig, A. S. (1988). Teacher re-creation of negative interactions with toddlers. In A. S. Honig (Ed.), Optimizing early child care and education (Special issue). Early Child Development and Care, 30.

James L. Hoot

AUTOBIOGRAPHICAL SKETCH OF
JAMES L. HOOT

After receiving his undergraduate degree in Psychology (1972), James Hoot taught primary grade children in a parochial school. To further his professional goals, in 1973 he joined the Virginia Teacher Corps Consortium where he taught Kindergarten children in rural Chesterfield County and the city of Richmond while pursuing a Masters Degree in Early Childhood Education. Following this, he pursued and achieved a Ph.D. in Early Childhood Education from the University of Illinois. Post-doctoral study in Computer Science was undertaken while a member of the Early Childhood Education faculty at North Texas State University, Denton, Texas.

For the past decade, Dr. Hoot's primary areas of interest have involved: (1) developing more effective programs for involving the rapidly growing elderly population in the education of children (2) exploring promises and problems technology (especially computer technology) holds for the very young and (3) developing a more universal awareness of the critical importance of educational play in the lives of children.

Dr. Hoot's interest in issues and concerns regarding the role of technology in the educational lives of children resulted in his volumes Computers in Early Childhood Education: Issues and Practices (Prentice-Hall, 1986) and Writing With Computers in the Early Grades, (with Steve Silvern, Teacher's College Press, 1988). In addition, he has been invited to share his work with computers and children in the Soviet Union, Israel, and Canada.

Many of Dr. Hoot's concerns regarding the education of children have been especially nurtured by scholars at the University of Illinois (Urbana) -- especially Bernard Spodek, who has made countless contributions to the field and to his students, and Lillian Katz. He has also been particularly influenced by the works of Seymour Papert who has raised serious concerns about the potential use of technology for developing young minds.

Dr. Hoot is currently Director of the Early Childhood Research Center at the State University of New York at Buffalo. Current research interests involve improving intergenerational understandings by bringing school children into contact with competent elderly computer tutors. He is also developing a project designed to use computer technology to build more constructive links between children of the U.S. and the U.S.S.R. His most recent volume is an activities-oriented volume (with Bernard Spodek and Olivia Saracho) designed to assist early childhood teachers in developing a play curriculum.

A TECHNOLOGICAL CHALLENGE
FOR EARLY CHILDHOOD PROFESSIONALS

Over a decade ago, I was first exposed to the world of computers. As a graduate student, I dutifully punched seemingly endless piles of cards to feed into that amorphous technological giant. While performing these duties, I recall seeing little relevance of these activities for the educational lives of children in my kindergarten/primary grade classes. (I also vividly recall feeling that I never wanted to touch a computer keyboard again).

In the late 70's, with the logrithmic expansion of personal computer use brought on by diminishing prices and increasing power of computers, my feelings toward these machines required a change. After inundating university and secondary curricular programs, the search for additional markets to accommodate the rise in competition among computer companies quickly brought computers into the price range of even preschool programs. These market forces, buttressed by unsubstantiated media claims, induced parents and teachers to purchase computers for even the youngest of children. By the mid-1980's, estimates suggested that computers were already in 25% of the preschool programs. In spite of a dearth of data, computers are rapidly becoming as common as blocks in programs for young children. If we are to maximize educational potential and minimize possible technological hazards, tremendous efforts are needed from the research arena.

As we approach the 1990's, the dust caused by the excessive claims of technological zealots of the past decade is beginning to settle. Informed parents no longer select programs for their children solely because of advertisements which herald "computer tutor experiences" designed to make their youngsters ready for later academic activities. Neither does the media now so emphatically perpetuate the unsupported message that parents who care for their children and want them to succeed in later schooling should provide them with a personal computer.

In addition to a more realistic view of computers held by the general public, teachers of young children are now more cognizant of technology-related issues. Perhaps the most serious of these issues lies in the area of computer software programs for the very young. To date, the preponderance of software for the very young has been of poor and of highly questionable quality. Specifically, programs have dealt with the simplest of concepts (especially math) and have been little more than workbooks on screens. Furthermore, these programs have been beset with inaccuracies, often sexist, seldom field tested, and they are frequently developed by authors with little or no knowledge of child growth and development. Despite enthusiastic claims of program developers, such software appears to accomplish little more than consume precious moments of children's lives.

In spite of the poor condition of most early childhood software, however, a couple of programs are beginning to show some educational promise -- Logo and word processing. Logo is a highly sophisticated graphics-oriented programming language developed specifically for children. Thus far, it has been shown that children as young as five can program with this language. (It should be noted here, however, that while research has shown that children can program with Logo, it remains to be determined the extent, if any, this program should be utilized in the early childhood curriculum.) Logo research has also demonstrated that, with the support of a competent teacher, Logo can facilitate development of specific metacognitive abilities. While promising, much additional research is needed before widescale employment of Logo in the early childhood curriculum.

In addition to Logo, word processing has also begun to show promise with children just breaking into print. With even minimal typing skills, children can use a computer as a typewriter to eliminate a great deal of the mechanical drudgery traditionally associated with writing. Rapidly developing voice-input variations of these programs allow users to create text without the use of even keyboards. Such programs, specifically designed for the very young, offer promise as tools to facilitate written communication.

Despite the potential beginning to emerge from Logo and word processing research, the field remains in desperate need of a better developed body of quality research exploring the potential impact of computers upon all areas of child development. It is especially important that such research transcends the impact of computers upon cognitive/academic outcomes. Equally important is research exploring the impact of technology upon self-confidence, motivation and the cultivation of those personal characteristics likely to result in more caring and understanding human beings.

The computer has made great strides toward shrinking the world. Might it be that as our world shrinks, this same technological device could be used as a tool to improve relationships among children of the world? (This question was frequently posed at the recent meeting of the Second International Congress on Early Childhood Education, Tel Aviv, Israel, 1987. Similar concerns have also led to the recent establishment of a special interest group by the International Council on Computers in Education.) Modems and other developing devices could be used to link users at all levels from all parts of the country and the world. Increased contacts supported by an effective teacher could promote better understandings among children as well as develop desired academic skills.

Computer linkages described above might also be able to improve human relationships on a more local level. One area of particular need concerns the diminishing contacts between very young and the elderly. With increased mobility and the emergence of numerous family forms, children have fewer contacts with older adults. It is quite possible, then, that educators could create opportunities in which very young children and older adults could be linked in a meaningful sort of way through computer technology. While these relatively inexpensive devices are readily available, intergenerational technological research is nearly non-existent.

In the above, I have suggested that computers are likely to consume increasing moments of the educational lives of young children. I have also suggested that, while a few programs appear promising, the majority of software programs for children are of questionable quality. Finally, I have suggested a future direction for the use of the computer as a tool for improving international and intergenerational understandings.

In conclusion, in spite of the lack of research data, administrators and curriculum builders from nearly every state are busy designing computer objectives for children beginning with kindergarten. The challenge I leave for readers of this volume is to begin exploration of the relative impact of computers upon all areas of children's lives.

Such research is likely to assist teachers of young children in molding existing computer objectives to conform with justifiable practice. Without a greatly expanded research base, however, inappropriate educational practices are likely to proliferate.

PUBLICATION BIBLIOGRAPHY

BOOKS:

Hoot, James L. and Steven Silvern, Editors, Writing With Computers in the Early Years, Teacher's College Press, 1988.

Hoot, James L., Editor, Computers in Early Childhood Education: Issues and Practices, Prentice-Hall, 1986.

CHAPTERS IN BOOKS:

Hoot, James L. and Sara Lundsteen, "Media and Other Resources in the Teaching of Language Arts." In Learning and Teaching Language Arts: A Problem Solving Approach, Sara W. Lundsteen, Editor, Harper, 1987.

Hoot, James L. "Computers in Early Childhood Education." In Computers in Early Childhood Education: Issues and Problems, James L. Hoot, Editor, Prentice-Hall, 1986.

Hoot, James L. and Jill Bardwell, "What's It Like?" In Guiding Young Children's Learning, Sara W. Lundsteen and N. Tarrow (eds). New York: McGraw-Hill, January, 1981.

ARTICLES:

Hoot, James L. and K. Hoag, "Kids, Keyboards and Computers: Issues and Ideas for Teachers." Day Care and Early Education, Vol. 14, No. 4 (Summer) 1987.

Hoot, James L. "Computing in the Soviet Union." The Computing Teacher, May, 1987.

Hoot, James L. "Keyboarding Instruction in the Early Grades: Must or Mistake?" Childhood Education, Vol. 63, 1987.

Johnson, M. and Hoot, James L. "Computers and the Classroom Teacher," Educational Horizons, Vol. 64, No. 2 (Winter, 1986), p. 73-75.

Hoot, James L. and Susan Anderson, "Kids, Carpentry, and the Preschool Classroom." Day Care and Early Education, Vol. 13, No. 3, (Spring, 1986) pp. 12-15.

Hoot, James L. "Computers in Child Care: Costs, Concerns and an Alternative." Texas Child Care Quarterly, Fall, 1984.

76

Hoot, James L. "A Computer for Children: Don't Worry If You Don't Have One." Adventure Years Digest, November, 1984.

Hoot, James L. "Computers in Early Childhood Education: Promises and Problems." Viewpoints, 120, October 10, 1983.

Hoot, James L. "Microcomputers in Early Childhood Education: Educational Promise and Problems." ERIC Clearinghouse on Elementary and Early Childhood Education, ED 235 897, October, 1984.

Hoot, James L. "Improving the Education of Very Young Children and Boosting University Enrollment Through a Masters Degree Program in Child Care Administration." ERIC Clearinghouse on Early Childhood Education, ED 242 424, February, 1983.

Hoot, James L. "Microcomputers and the Elderly: New Directions for Self-sufficiency and Life-Long Learning." Educational Gerontology: An International Bi-Monthly, Vol. 9, Nos. 5-6, Sept.-Dec. 1983, pp. 493-499.

Rubens, T., J. Hoot and J. Poole, "Introducing Microcomputers to Micro-Learners Through Play." Day Care and Early Education, Vol. 11, No. 3, Spring, 1984, pp. 29-31.

Hoot, James L. "Senior Citizens: The Untapped Resource for Improving Programs for Young Children." The Learner in Process, Vol. 5, No. 1, Winter, 1984, p. 11-14.

Hoot, James L. "CAUTION: A Decrease in Play May Be Hazardous to Children's School Success," The Texas Child Care Quarterly, Vol. 8, No. 1, Summer, 1984, pp. 10-13.

Hoot, James L. "Microcomputers for the Micro-Learner: Educational Promise," The Learner in Process, Vol. 4, No. 2, Spring, 1983.

Hoot, James L. "Older Adult Volunteers," Day Care and Early Education, Vol. 10, No. 3, Spring, 1983.

Hoot, James L. "Learning - A Moving Experience," Early Years, Vol. 13, No. 7, March, 1983.

Hoot, James L. and Lance M. Gentile, "Kindergarten Play: The Foundation of Reading," The Reading Teacher, Vol. 36, No. 4, January, 1983.

Hoot, James L., "Strengthening Head Start Classrooms Through Elderly Involvement." Among, U. S. Journal of the National Head Start Association, Spring, 1983.

Hoot, James L. "Gray Power: The Untapped Resource for Improving Programs for Young Children," Early Childhood Education Options, Vol. VII, No. 4, May, 1982.

Hoot, James L. "The Public Schools and Teaching About Aging," Educational Gerontology: An International Quarterly, Vol. 6, December, 1982.

77

Hoot, James L. and D. Barry Lumsden, "Aging Education in the Texas Public Schools -- Coming of Age." ERIC Clearinghouse on Teacher Education, Washington D.C., SP 017657, ED 199233, 1981.

Hoot, James L. "Reflection in Student Teaching." Cornbelt Educational Review, University of Illinois, June, 1977.

Hoot, James L. and William E. Ade. "Parent Involvement: Motivation vs. Alienation," Day Care and Early Education, November/December, 1976.

Hoot, James L. "Henry Gets A Heart." Early Years, March, 1976.

Hoot, James L. "Jerry and Jean -- What Have You Done?" Dimensions, October, 1975.

James L. Hymes, Jr.

AUTOBIOGRAPHICAL SKETCH OF
JAMES L. HYMES

James L. Hymes' dedication to the education of young children spans many decades. He was born in New York City and earned degrees from Teachers College at Columbia, Harvard and finally a Doctor of Education degree from Columbia. He supervised nursery schools for the Works Progress Administration as his first job. One of his earlier experiences that continues to be historically significant was his directorship of the Kaiser Child Study Centers in Portland, Oregon during World War II. The advent of the war caused women to leave the home and assume traditionally male dominated jobs. One problem that resulted from mothers working was providing care for their youngsters. Day care centers, as we know them today, were unavailable because the majority of women remained at home to care for their own children. Under the Lanham Act, the federal government provided money to build and staff child care centers for those mothers who joined the work force during World War II. Two centers that served as models for that period of time and today continue to reflect the quality of child care that can result when the need is critical included the two shipyard Kaiser centers that Dr. Hymes directed. Mothers felt secure about taking their children with them to work and knowing they were safe and well cared for at the child care center near them. These centers were open twenty-four hours a day to accommodate the different shifts of work at the shipyard. Industry soon learned that happy mothers became more productive workers. Many leading educators today believe the Kaiser project has not yet been equalled in terms of functionalism and excellence. This endeavor serves as a model for what can be done for the case of children when the need is critical, when ample money is available and when knowledgeable directors for child care programs are in leadership roles.

After the war and the closing of the child care centers, Dr. Hymes accepted a professorship in education at New York State University at New Paltz. In 1949, he joined the education department at George Peabody College. In 1957, Dr. Hymes became Professor of Education at the University of Maryland and remained there until his retirement in 1970.

The years since Dr. Hymes' retirement have continued to be filled with his ardent struggle to improve the lives of children. He has traveled and lectured throughout the country presenting solid guidance to caregivers of children. His writings and publications are notable and reflect his philosophy of humane educational progress for young children that are free of rigid adult-structured standards. Dr. Hymes is past president of the National Association for the Education of Young Children. He has been the recipient of many honors that include the SACUS Award of Recognition in 1970.

Dr. Hymes currently lives in Carmel, California. He is the father of three children and the grandfather of many. He still continues to speak out for children.

The Editors

A LIFE IN EARLY CHILDHOOD EDUCATION

My involvement with young children began in 1934. In '34 and '35 I was a graduate assistant at the Child Development Institute at Teachers College, Columbia. A part of my job included recording the behavior of the children in the Institute's Nursery School.

Upon receiving my master's degree in Child Development and Parent Education in 1936, I then worked for two years in New York state as one of the supervisors in the federally supported WPA nursery schools.

From then on my work brought me in touch with the many varied fields in Early Childhood Education. I was the director of a private experimental school, a "co-op" serving two-year-olds up to the junior high age. During World War II, I was the director of the largest (and, I think, best) child care program, the two Child Service Centers at the Kaiser shipyards in Portland, Oregon. I was the head of the Early Childhood Program at what is now New York State University at New Paltz. Here we developed the first program of teacher training for the state's new Early Childhood Certificate, covering the years of three through eight. I held a similar position at George Peabody College for Teachers in Nashville, and following that at the University of Maryland. At Maryland, I was also the Director of the University school which served children ages two through five. While at Maryland, I served on the National Planning Committee which set up Head Start and, on a six-month leave of absence from the University, worked in the Washington Head Start headquarters to help the program get under way.

81

I resigned from the University of Maryland in 1970, frustrated by the University's failure (as I saw it) to seize its opportunities for leadership in Early Childhood. Moving to California in semi-retirement, I became a free-lance consultant in Early Childhood: Lecturer, workshop leader, short-course teacher, etc. In this period I gave a great deal of time to the preparation and editing of more than 70 tapes and slide-tape presentations about Early Childhood for use in teacher education.

As I write this in 1987, fifty-three years from the start, I am still involved in Early Childhood Education, now as the owner-editor-promotions manager-sole author-office boy-total staff of Hacienda Press in Carmel, California. Our present "best-sellers": Notes for Parents and the annual Early Childhood Education -- The Year in Review. A Look at 1987 will be the seventeenth yearly report in that series.

How did all this begin? During my high school and college years, I was a summer camp counselor working with what we all thought of as "very young" children, ages eight to twelve. I have to add, immodestly: I was a very good counselor. When I graduated in 1934 from Harvard College with a major in International Relations, I -- along with many, many others in the Depression -- was jobless. The camp director at the time -- a man who became my great, good friend and main professional advisor -- Dr. Ernest G. ("Lank") Osborne, urged me to study at the TC Child Development Institute where he was the specialist in Parent Education. It was there I met really young children, in the Institute's nursery school.

Lank was the first of many wonderful humans and outstanding educational leaders with whom I had the good fortune to be associated. The Director of the Child Development Institute was Lois Meek Stolz, first President of NAEYC. Our friendship began in 1935 when I was her Graduate Assistant; grew closer in 1943-1945 when the two of us worked together at the Kaiser Child Service Centers and became closer still when our family moved, in 1970, to California where she then lived. The friendship persisted until her death at age 93 in 1985.

My good fortune in working with top-flight people continued when I left the Institute to work with the WPA nursery schools in Albany, New York. There my boss was Dr. Ruth Andrus, another early leader in child development and nursery school movements. Following Albany, I worked with the Progressive Education Association as Editor of the magazine, Progressive Education, and as managing Editor of its exciting companion, the left-leaning social commentary, Frontiers of Democracy. These positions let me know, at a very young age, the men and women who were the "movers and shakers" in sensitive, child-centered education.

Through the years, my role revolved largely around the effort to communicate to parents, teachers, administrators and the general public the characteristics of young children and how their needs could best be met at home and in groups. To this end I have done a great deal of writing: many magazine articles for parents and teachers, several books, and a goodly number of pamphlets. Copies of all my publications, as well as many teaching and lecture notes and some correspondence, are on file in the Arichives of Pacific Oaks College, Pasadena, California. I have tended to concentrate on pamphlets: short, easy to read, with no pedagese, and inexpensive. Even my books meet these standards. I have always been proud that two of my short books, Behavior and Misbehavior, and A Child Development Point of View, were the first paperbacks in education. (Prentice-Hall once sold them, 2 for 99 cents! I thought that was carrying the point a little far.)

Learning to write simply -- it was not a natural "gift", but a product of never-ending editing and re-writing -- began with my doctoral dissertation. When the Kaiser program ended at the close of World War II, I worked on a fellowship for six months at the Caroline Zachry Institute of Human Development, headed at that time by Lawrence K. Frank, a brilliant, creative man who had been involved in every significant development in the early childhood, parent education and mental health fields. It was he who suggested using the idea of the "war babies" coming to school as a tool to sensitize adults to children's needs. The result: A Pound of Prevention--How Teachers Can Meet the Emotional Needs of Young Children, a paperback which sold more than a million copies (!), an unusual record for a dissertation. (I hasten to add: This was a non-profit operation!)

Another mass-distribution (also non-profit) publication: I wrote and the U.S. Government Printing Office published A Healthy Personality for your Child, a distillation of the framework developed at the Mid-Century White House Conference on Children and Youth by Eric Erickson.

In the course of 53 years, I taught and lectured about Early Childhood Education in 47 of our 50 states (including, to my pleasure, both Hawaii and Alaska). One experience I especially welcomed: In 1961, I taught a twice-a-week half-hour class on "The Child Under Six" over the CBS television stations in Washington, D.C. and Baltimore. I followed that with two years as "The Story Man", a volunteer effort in which I read for fifteen minutes from the field's best children's literature to an audience that reportedly ran from age one to ninety-one!

Children's literature, not surprisingly, has been a continuous interest. The greatest challenge I faced in writing were the books I wrote for children: sixteen paperbacks published by Row, Peterson: The Books To Start On (4 of them) and the Books To Stretch On (the Bingo Series, six of them and the Chuckle Series, six more). All aimed to help young children learn to read but to go about that task with a great deal of pleasure. These were real books -- not "school" books -- with honest-to-goodness plots (not namby-pamby foolishness). They were simple little books and, because of that, so hard to write! Unfortunately, they were also "artistic failures" -- based on wonderful ideas, but very, very few children ever saw them. (I think because selling them, one to a classroom, brought in no money for the book salesman.)

Collaborating with my wife, Lucia, two other children's books were more successful: Hooray for Chocolate and Other Easy-to-Read Jingles and Oodles of Noodles and Other Hymes Rhymes. These, intended to be bought by parents rather than by schools, reached a larger audience (thank heavens).

Some reflections as I look back on this lifetime of work: one personal satisfaction stands out: my enjoyment in my associations with college students, with parents, with young children. One great worry is present: young children are, I think, more vulnerable today than ever. The high percentage of mothers in the labor force plus our failure to provide good child care facilities is very frightening. The lack of top-quality public child care centers added to the mass of single parent homes, poverty, and the stresses of modern life all threaten young children. As I look back, I know one professional joy: the number of public kindergartens for fives and now increasingly for four-year-olds, too and the number of private nursery schools have greatly increased since 1934. Also, today we have Head Start which, while small in size and seemingly stuck in its small size, represents an addition in number. But as I look back, I am very aware of one great failure: while the number of programs has increased, the quality of programs has not. The struggle against over-structured, adult-dominated, paper-and-pencil, insensitive, tense and stressful classrooms goes on. These were the curse of 1934; they are the curse of 1987. But this long-standing danger is more severe today because more children are exposed to it and because today's children are so very open to hurt.

PUBLICATION BIBLIOGRAPHY

BOOKS:

1952. Understanding Your Child. Englewood Cliffs, NJ: Prentice-Hall. (Published in London, 1954; translated into Swedish, 1969; Spanish, 1971.)

1953. Effective Home-School Relations. Englewood Cliffs, NJ: Prentice-Hall. Revised edition: 1974, Hacienda Press, Carmel, CA.

1955. A Child Development Point of View. Englewood Cliffs, NJ: Prentice-Hall. Republished: 1977, Greenwood Press, Westport, CT.

1955. Behavior and Misbehavior. Englewood Cliffs, NJ: Prentice-Hall. Republished: 1977, Greenwood Press, Westport, CT.

1958. Before The Child Reads. New York: Harper and Row.

1963. The Child Under Six. Englewood Cliffs, NJ: Prentice-Hall. (Translated into Swedish, 1965; Portuguese, 1966.)

1968. Teaching the Child Under Six. Columbus, OH: Charles E. Merrill. (2nd edition, 1968; 3rd edition, 1981.

CHAPTERS IN BOOKS:

1947. Parents, Ch. II in Intercultural Attitudes in the Making, William H. Kilpatrick, ed. New York: Harper.

1952. The Beginning of Education, Ch. 6 in Our Children Today, Sidonie Gruenberg, ed. New York: Viking Press.

1953. Better Humans, Better Citizens, Ch XV in The American Elementary School, Harold Shane, ed. John Dewey Society Yearbook, New York: Harper.

1954. Early Steps in Growing Up, Ch 11 in Encyclopedia of Child Care and Guidance, Sidonie Gruenberg, ed. New York: Doubleday.

1956. Helping Parents Understand Children, in Education 2000 A.D., Lance Hunnicutt, Ed., Syracuse: Syracuse University Press.

1956. The Child in Modern Society, Ch. 6 in Great Human Issues of our Times. Nashville: George Peabody College for Teachers.

1960. Starting with a Child, Ch. 6 in Those First School Years. Washington: Department of Elementary School Principals, NEA.

Also: Entries on Nursery School, Kindergarten, The Child in World Book Encyclopedia. Chicago: Field Enterprises.

BOOKS FOR CHILDREN:

1955. Books To Stretch On (a series of 12). Evanston: Row, Peterson.

1959. Books To Start On (a series of 4). Evanston: Row, Peterson.

1960. Hooray for Chocolate (with Lucia Manley Hymes). New York: William R. Scott.

1964. Oodles of Noodles (with Lucia Manley Hymes). New York: William R. Scott.

PAMPHLETS:

1949. Being a Good Parent. New York: TC Bureau of Publications. (Translated into Japanese, 1955; Spanish, 1957.)

1949. Discipline. New York: TC Bureau of Publications. (Translated in Japanese, 1955; Spanish, 1957.)

1949. Teacher Listen, The Children Speak. New York: New York State Committee for Mental Health.

1949. Enjoy Your Child: Ages 1,2,3. New York: Public Affairs Committee. (Translated into German; 1959; Turkish, 1964. Reprinted in The Growing Family, Maxwell Stewart, ed. New York: Harper and Row, 1955.

1950. A Pound of Prevention. New York: New York State Committee for Mental Health. (Published in Oxford, Eng., 1953 by Lincombe Lodge Research Library.)

1950. A Good Nursery School in Your Free Public School. Washington: National Association for the Education of Young Children.

1950. Why Have Nursery Schools. Washington: National Association for the Education of Young Children.

1950. How To Tell Your Child About Sex. New York: Public Affairs Committee. Reprinted in The Growing Family, Maxwell Stewart, ed. New York: Harper and Row, 1955.

1950. Three to Six: Your Child Starts to School. New York: Public Affairs Committee. Reprinted in The Growing Family, Maxwell Stewart, ed. New York: Harper and Row, 1955.

1952. A Healthy Personality for Your Child. Washington: Government Printing Office.

1953. An Evaluation of the Basic Readers for the School Beginner, Monograph #29. Evanston: Row, Peterson.

1954. How Are the Fives Faring In Your Town? Washington: Association for Childhood Education International.

1960. Public Kindergartens. Washington: National Education Association.

1968. Early Childhood Education: An Introduction to the Profession. Washington: NAEYC. 2nd ed. 1975.

1971. Early Childhood Education: The Year in Review. An annual. Carmen, CA: Hacienda Press.

1985. Worth Repeating -- Kindergarten Briefs. (From The Grade Teacher, 1958-1965.) Carmel, CA: Hacienda Press.

Mary Renck Jalongo

AUTOBIOGRAPHICAL SKETCH OF
MARY RENCK JALONGO

Mary Renck Jalongo is a Professor of Education and Director of the Doctoral Program in Elementary Education at Indiana University of Pennsylvania. In 1983, she was named Pennsylvania's Outstanding Young Woman. In 1985, Dr. Jalongo received a best essay award from the Association for the Study of Higher Education for an article entitled "Faculty Productivity in Higher Education", published in The Educational Forum. Other manuscripts she has authored have appeared in Childhood Education, Young Children, The Reading Teacher, PTA Today, Scholarly Publishing, and School Library Journal. In addition, Dr. Jalongo is a Professional Development consultant for Phi Delta Kappa International and is the 1988 inductee for the Gabbard Institute on Professional Writing. Her editorial board service includes The Association for Childhood Education International, the National Association for the Education of Young Children, and Human Sciences Press. Areas of interest and expertise include literature for young children, social and emotional development during early childhood, the professional development of educators, and writing for publication. Dr. Jalongo earned an undergraduate degree in English and Spanish at Mercy College of Detroit, a Master of Arts in Teaching from Oakland University, and a Ph.D. in Early Childhood Education and Research from the University of Toledo.

MENTORS, MASTER TEACHERS
AND TEACHER INDUCTION

While waiting at the airport gate to board my flight, I watched a carrot-topped toddler making his way around two rows of chairs. He was staying close to his mother until he noticed a teenager with flame orange cock's comb hairstyle. The child looked up at the young man, rested a chubby hand on his knee and then began to speak in that blend of jibberish and conversation characteristic of his age. The adolescent smiled, leaned over, and said softly, "Like the hair, huh?" After making several tactile comparisons between his own soft ringlets and stiff tuft of teenage hair, the toddler ran back to his mother, crowing with delight over his adventure. As a teacher educator, I wanted to know more about this young man. Based upon that brief observation, he seemed to have five qualities which are essential to excellence in teaching: spontaneity, perceptivity, decision-making, creativity and flexibility (Rubin, 1985).

Whenever I read this list of attributes, I get worried. Who teaches these things to a prospective teacher? Even the best teacher preparation programs develop rather than introduce these elements. Content can be taught, methods can be taught, but those things which elevate teaching to an art must be learned long before the freshman year of college.

The preparation of a teacher begins during childhood and lasts a lifetime. Often the child's first teacher figures prominently in this process. It is my anecdotal impression that people can recall the name of their first teacher long after the names of many others have been forgotten. Let me tell you about mine.

I spent the entire morning of my first day of kindergarten seated on a wooden horse. Unlike the merry-go-round stallions or the mechanical saddle horse at the A & P, it was homely, stationary and constructed from a barrel. Although it was not a very comfortable seat, it enabled me to see the entire classroom without feeling any pressure to participate. At recess time, my teacher waited until the other children filed out before inviting me to come outside and see the playground. I climbed down. On that day and in the weeks that followed, I recognized that Miss Klingensmith was competent, caring and insightful. When I played school, which was often, I always insisted on being Miss Klingensmith. That early experience touches my life deeply even now.

I see the preparation of teachers as an upward spiral, a process that begins and ends with role models. First the child admires and emulates good teachers. Then the adolescent or adult decides to become a good teacher and, having done so, becomes a role model for other teachers. At each stage in this cycle, people need the same basic things from their role models: advocacy, validation, guidance and support. They need mentors. Mentoring is far from being a new idea, but mentor/protege relationships are a contemporary issue in education.

Mentorships in Education

Many states and the school districts within them have implemented, or are about to institute, teacher induction programs (Lawney, 1986). In most mentor teacher plans, beginning teachers will serve a one-year apprenticeship with a master teacher. There is, however, a serious oversight in many of these programs. Although role models are essential, they cannot be legislated, assigned or even elected. There are at least three reasons why this is so, and all of them have to do with the mentoring dynamic:

1. Mentors are relatively rare. Mentors have been described as competent, dedicated, accessible, open, autonomous, powerful, fair, trustworthy, motivated and held in high esteem (Erkut & Mokros, 1984). Mentors are, to use Maslow's (1970) terminology, self-actualized. They have met their own needs for personal/professional growth. They are both able and willing to contribute to the personal/professional growth of others. Thus, the assumption that all or even most teachers will become mentors is clearly erroneous. Equally misguided is the notion that educators suffering from "burn out" can be transformed into mentors by completing an inservice training program which teaches them "the skills of mentoring". Mentorship is not a skill. It is an interpersonal dynamic between two skilled individuals.

If anything, mentorship in education is doubly difficult. Mentors must be highly successful in teaching children. They must be highly effective in working with adult learners as well. This need to excel with two different age groups adds to the demands of the mentoring role.

2. The mentor-protege relationship is complex. Consider for a moment the origins of the word protege. It is a Latin derivative which means "protected". Mentors protect proteges (and proteges are loyal to their mentors) because they identify with one another. The mentor thinks, "This person is like me in some ways, a good student striving to become a good teacher, but needing someone to guide, support and encourage along the way." The protege thinks, "Here is a person I want to emulate -- someone who has already achieved what I aspire to. If this person believes in me, it helps me to have confidence in myself." Not surprisingly, most mentors were once proteges themselves (O'Neil, 1981). In studies of the mentoring process, mentors often report feeling indebted to give others the same kind of help they needed and received as beginning professionals (Elliott & Holmbert-Wright, 1983).

3. Mentoring is exclusionary. One of the difficulties in research on mentoring is that causation has not been established (Merriam, 1983). Mentoring does not lend itself to experimental research designs because it is a complex social process. Despite these problems, this question still remains: Do mentors contribute significantly to their proteges' careers or do they simply have an eye for talent which would emerge without their intervention? It does appear that proteges who

91

have one mentor can usually attract more and that mentors usually work with several proteges during their professional lives (Sandler & Hall, 1983). Evidently, both parties possess characteristics which are recognized and valued by fellow professionals.

Mentoring and Teacher Education

Applying these concepts to teacher education raises many questions. Perhaps the most important are:

How may mentor teachers be identified and how many could be reasonably expected to exist in a school or district?

Are all beginning teachers "mentorable"? If not, how should proteges be selected?

What will be done to insure a successful match between mentors and proteges?

One reason why teacher education has been barraged by criticism is that teaching is not selective enough. This situation has been discussed at great length elsewhere (Task Force on Teaching as a Profession, 1986). Unfortunately, many of the proposed solutions are quantitative -- more credits, different courses, tougher assignments and standardized tests. All of these recommendations, while worthy of consideration, are doomed to fall short of achieving excellence in education. It is like defining a good driver as someone who can read the Snelling Eye chart and memorize enough traffic rules to pass a multiple-choice item test. One of the few qualitative recommendations for teacher education reform is the mentor teacher concept. Returning to the driver's license analogy, teacher induction becomes a road test and the mentor teacher, a driving instructor. Should the instructor become the examiner as well, the person who will decide whether a certificate is conferred? Most classroom teachers are opposed, and rightly so, to this "eleventh hour" mixture of supervisory and evaluative function. Selection and rigor should be exercised before induction while the student still has the option of changing majors and careers. It should be pointed out that while mentors in other fields do evaluate, this evaluation does not pose a problem because proteges are carefully selected and are therefore unlikely to fail.

So far, this discussion of mentoring has made it sound

haphazard. It is possible, however, to make mentoring systematic and retain the essential attributes of the process.

Mentorship Programs

A planned mentoring program would function something like this:

1. Teachers apply and interview to become mentors. Applications should include evidence of teaching ability (such as a videotape of their teaching, peer/administrator observations), endorsements of their former student teachers (where available), documentation of professional activities (such as mini grant proposals) and community service. A panel composed of colleagues, administrators and community members would review these materials, interview the applicants and make their selections.

2. Mentors are prepared for their role. Even though mentoring is considered to be the pinnacle of interpersonal effectiveness and largely something that those selected already possess, an orientation and an ongoing forum for the discussion of mentor/protege issues is important. I view this as an orientation rather than as training. Whereas training tends to emphasize knowledge and skills, preparation for mentoring would build knowledge and skills but emphasize attitudes and values. The knowledge and skills to be built would include an orientation to the specific program, a thorough background in adult learning theory and familiarity with research on beginning teachers (see Gray & Gray, 1985). Applications of this theoretical and research base could then be applied to simulations of mentor-protege interaction and to observations of successful mentors at work. Most importantly, mentor teacher preparation should provide opportunities for mentor teachers to function in a collegial way with other mentors, administrators and university faculty. Collaborative action research involving universities and public schools would be one possibility for enhancing the professional growth of mentors (Ward, 1984).

3. College graduates apply and interview to become inductees. After the mentor teachers are identified, their first responsibility would be to select the inductees. This should not be viewed as usurping the power of the administration. It is a legitimate, crucial function of mentors to select their proteges. Following the interviews, each mentor would choose a person to sponsor. The protege would then be notified of the mentor's interest and be invited to observe in the mentor's

classroom before formally accepting the position. After the program is in place, systematic evaluation should be carried out.

The system outlined here may be more complicated than an "open door" policy, but it will certainly result in a higher success rate. It gives mentors greater autonomy than other approaches. It does not confuse colleagueship (which is interaction among professionals with equal status) with mentorship (which is a hierarchical type of interaction between novice and accomplished professionals). It encourages districts to recruit early and plan well. Most importantly, It does not violate the essential elements of mentoring in the interest of expedience.

American education does not have a particularly distinguished history with handling powerful ideas -- progressive education, open education, team teaching, individualized instruction and the process approach to writing, to name a few. Mentoring is more than a rung on a career ladder or a three-day inservice program It is also more than a group of veteran teachers stealing a few moments to help out a beginning teacher. Mentor teacher programs will take time and cost money. But if education can manage to preserve the concept's integrity, mentoring may well be the single most valuable strategy for elevating the status of the teaching profession and promoting excellence in our schools.

SELECTED PUBLICATIONS

Jalongo, M. R. (1987). On the compatibility of teaching and scholarly writing. Scholarly Publishing. (in press).

Jalongo, M. R. & Zeigler, S. (1987). Writing in kindergarten and first grade. Childhood Education. (in press).

Jalongo, M. R. (1987). Normal childhood fears. PTA Today. (in press).

Jalongo, M. R. & Renck, M. A. (1987). Children's literature and the process of school adjustment. The Reading Teacher, 40 (7): 616-623.

Jalongo, M. R. (1987). Do "security" blankets belong in preschool? Young Children, 42, 3-8.

Jalongo, M. R. (1987). Videocasettes for children. PTA Today, 12, 16-18.

Jalongo, M. R. (1986). "What is happening to Kindergarten?" Childhood Education, 63, 154-160 (adopted as position paper on kindergarten by New York State Board of Education).

Jalongo, M. R. (1986). Childhood fears and children's literature. Bulletin of the Children's Literature Assembly of NCTE, 12, 2-5.

Brown, L. & Jalongo, M. R. (1986). Parent-teacher conferences. PTA Today, 12, 14-16.

Brown, L., Jalongo, M. R. & Mills, S. E. (1985/1986). What everyone should know about adoption. PTA Today, 11, 19-20.

Brown, L., Jalongo, M. R. & McCracken, J. B. (1985). Writing for publication in early childhood education. An article-length brochure published by the National Association for the Education of Young Children and in the journal, Young Children , 41 (2): 19-23.

Brown, L., Jalongo, M. R. (1985). Faculty productivity in higher education. The Educational Forum, (Winter), 171-182.

Brown, L, Jalongo, M. R. (1985). When young children move. Young Children, 40, 51-57.

Jalongo, M. R. (1985). Children's literature: There's some sense to its humor. Childhood Education, 62, 109-114.

Jalongo, M. R. & Collins, M. (1985). Singing with children! Folk music for nonmusicians. Young Children, 40, 17-22.

Jalongo, M. R. & Renck, M. A. (1985). Sibling relationships: A recurrent developmental and literary theme. Childhood Education, 61, 346-351.

Jalongo, M. R. & Renck, M. A. (1985). Stories that sing. School Library Journal, 32, 42-43.

Jalongo, M. R. (1985). Choosing and using crisis-oriented materials with young children. Beginnings, 2, 27-30.

Jalongo, M. R. (1985). Siblings: Can they, will they, ever get along? PTA Today, 10, 16-19. (Reprinted in Social Issues Resources Series, The Family).

Jalongo, M. R. (1984). Imaginary companions in children's lives and literature. Childhood Education, 60, 166-171.

Jalongo, M. R. & Bromley, K. D. (1984). Developing linguistic competence through picture books. The Reading Teacher, 37, 840-845.

D'Angelo, K. A. & Jalongo, M. R. (1984). Song picture books and the language disabled child. Teaching Exceptional Children, 16, 114-120.

Jalongo, M. R. (1984). Children's fantasy: Childhood is the time to live splendidly as a child. PTA Today, 10, 7-10.

Jalongo, M. R. (1984). The top ten: Song picture books. The Bulletin/Children's Literature Assembly of NCTE, 10, 4-5.

Jalongo, M. R. & Renck, M. A. (1984). Looking homeward: Nostalgia in children's literature. School Library Journal, 31, 36-39.

Jalongo, M. R. (1984). Make believe: What good is it? Newsletter of Parenting, 8, 8-9.

Jalongo, M. R. (1984). Children's imaginary companions. `Education Digest, 50, 43-45.

Jalongo, M. R. (1983). Promoting peer acceptance of the newly immigrated child. Childhood Education, 117-124.

Jalongo, M. R. (1983). Bibliotherapy: Literature to promote socioemotional growth. The Reading Teacher, 36, 796-803.

Jalongo, M. R. (1983). Using crisis-oriented books with young children. Young Children, 40, 29-36.

CHAPTERS IN BOOKS:

"When Young Children Move" and "Using Crisis-oriented Books with Young Children", articles selected as chapters for Reducing Stress in Young Children, Janet Brown McCracken, Editor, Washington, DC: National Association for the Education of Young Children, 1986.

"Peer Acceptance and the Newly Immigrated Child", an article selected as a chapter in "Readings From Childhood Education, Anne Eddowes and James Quisenberry, Editors. Washington, DC: Association for Childhood Education International (in press).

Constance Kamii

AUTOBIOGRAPHICAL SKETCH OF
CONSTANCE KAMII

I received a B.A. in sociology from Pomona College and an M.A. in education and a Ph.D. in education and psychology from the University of Michigan. I thus did not have any background in early childhood education, but my first job after the Ph.D. was as Research Associate of the Perry Preschool Program in Ypsilanti, Michigan. The Perry Preschool Program was an experimental project created to test the hypothesis that lower-class black children's likelihood of success in school could be improved by giving them two years of preschool education before kindergarten. However, no one in preschool education seemed to know how to conceptualize objectives except in terms of subjects such as reading and arithmetic, and isolated bits of knowledge such as the names of colors and geometric shapes. This state of affairs existed because no one seemed to have scientific knowledge of the knowledge of preschool children (in relation to what they knew in infancy and what they will know at ages 8, 19, 15, and beyond).

After examining every teaching method that existed in early childhood education and all the research and theories of cognition that I could find, I concluded that the only promising theory for the conceptualization of objectives was that of Jean Piaget. I thus spent 1966-67 and most of 1970-73 as a postdoctoral research fellow under Piaget, and continued studying under him for ten more years on a joint appointment with the University of Illinois at Chicago and the University of Geneva.

With Hermina Sinclair of the University of Geneva as my mentor and Rheta DeVries as a collaborator, I started working on the practical application of Piaget's theory to early childhood education. This work can be seen in <u>Physical Knowledge in Preschool Education</u> (1978), <u>Group Games in Early Education</u> (1980), and <u>Number in Preschool and Kindergarten</u> (1982). I subsequently started working in the primary grades and wrote <u>Young Children Reinvent Arithmetic</u> (1985).

I have been at the University of Alabama at Birmingham since 1984 working with 13 teachers in a public school to develop a primary math program based on Piaget's theory. A progress report will be published in a book entitled <u>Young Children Continue to Reinvent Arithmetic, 2nd Grade</u>. As can be seen in the following essay, I believe in light of Piaget's constructivism that children should be allowed to do

27 + 38, for example, through their own natural ability to think. They are now taught rules (algorithms) to follow without understanding them. Mechanically following incomprehensible rules that produce correct answers prevents the development of critical, independent thinking.

When autonomy is the aim of education in the teacher's mind, this goal changes almost everything he or she does in the classroom. I plan to continue working closely with teachers to figure out ways of changing teaching to foster the development of autonomy in children.

AUTONOMY OR HETERONOMY: OUR CHOICES OF GOALS

Do the following have anything in common: the Watergate coverup affair, the Nazi murder of millions of Jews, the mass suicides at Jonestown, and the current problems of drug abuse and teenage pregnancy? These phenomena may seem very different, but they share one element in common: heteronomy. Heteronomy means being governed by someone else. It is the opposite of autonomy, which means being governed by oneself. The point I would like to make in this paper is that educators ought to play a part in raising generations who are more autonomous.

I use the term autonomy here in the framework of Jean Piaget's (1932) theory. In this theory, autonomy means not the right but the ability to make decisions by taking relevant factors into account. Piaget distinguished between two aspects of autonomy, the moral and intellectual aspects. A good way to explain autonomy is by giving extreme examples.

An extreme example of moral autonomy is Martin Luther King's struggle for racial equality. Convinced that equality among the races was best for all concerned, he fought for this cause in spite of the sanctions against his struggle, such as the police, dogs, jails, and threats of assassination. Morally autonomous people are governed by their convictions about right and wrong, rather than by reward and punishment. An extreme example of intellectual autonomy is Nicolaus Copernicus' promulgation of the heliocentric theory. Everybody else in the 1540s believed that the sun revolved around the earth, and the scientists of his time jeered at him during his lectures. But Copernicus was autonomous enough to remain convinced of the truth of his ideas.

Is autonomy a personality trait (like aggressiveness) or a developmental stage? Piaget's answer to this question is that it is a developmental stage not attained by many adults. All babies are born helpless and unable to govern themselves. As they grow older, a few become relatively autonomous. The men in the Watergate affair remained heteronomous. They were governed by President Nixon and went along with what they knew to be morally wrong. If they had been able to take relevant factors into account, such as the welfare of their fellow citizens, they would not have complied with the President's wishes. When former Nazi officers are charged with their responsibility in the Holocaust, they typically say they were only obeying orders. They, too, are examples of heteronomy. On a smaller scale, the current drug problem is likewise a symptom of heteronomy. People who can take relevant factors into account do not decide to take drugs.

Why are so many people heteronomous? Piaget's answer to this question is that parents and educators reinforce children's natural heteronomy by using rewards and punishment, thereby preventing autonomy from developing. I will clarify this statement below, first in the moral realm and then in the intellectual realm.

Moral Autonomy

Most parents and educators are profoundly convinced that rewards and punishment are effective for teaching moral values. Punishment, however, leads to three possible outcomes. The most common one is calculation of risks. The child who is punished for telling a lie, for example, will repeat the same act but will try to avoid being caught the next time. Sometimes children stoically decide in advance that, even if they are caught, the pleasure that the act will bring will be worth the price. The second possible outcome of punishment is the opposite of the first one, namely blind conformity. Some sensitive children become total conformists because conformity assures them of security and respectability. As conformists, children no longer have to make decisions; all they have to do is obey. The third possible outcome of punishment is revolt. Some children, after years of angelic behavior, decide that they are tired of pleasing their parents and teachers all the time. and that the time has come for them to begin living for themselves. Such children may even begin to engage in various behaviors that charcterize delinquency. These behaviors may look like autonomous acts, but there is a vast difference between autonomy and revolt. In revolt, the individual is opposing conformity. Nonconformity

100

does not necessarily make an individual autonomous.

Punishment thus reinforces children's heteronomy and prevents them from developing autonomy. Although rewards are more pleasurable than punishment, they also reinforce children's heteronomy. Children who help their parents only to earn money or who study only to get good grades are governed by others, just as are children who behave well only to avoid being punished. Adults control children by using rewards and punishment, thereby keeping them heteronomous.

If we want children to develop autonomy, we must encourage them to construct moral values from within by exchanging points of view with them. For example, if a child tells a lie, the adult can respond by withholding dessert or by making him write 50 times "I will not lie." Alternatively, the adult can look the child straight in the eye and say, with a combination of skepticism and affection, "I really can't believe what you are saying because..." The child, seeing that the adult cannot believe him, can be motivated to think about what he must do to be believed. Given many similar opportunities over time, he is likely to arrive at the conviction that it is best, in the long run, for people to deal honestly with one another. The person who has constructed this conviction from within cannot obey a Richard Nixon, no matter what rewards are offered for lying to the public.

Piaget made an important distinction between punishment and sanctions by reciprocity. Punishment (such as the withdrawal of dessert in the above example) is unrelated to the act we want to sanction. By contrast, a sanction by reciprocity is directly related to the act. For instance, not being believed is a direct consequence of lying, and this direct relationship makes it possible for the child to think about what he must do to be believed. The reader is referred to Piaget (1932, Ch. 3) and Kamii (1984) for further detail about sanctions by reciprocity.

Parents and educators generally assume that children learn moral values by internalizing them from the environment, and that rewards and punishment help this internalization. It is true that some children appear to internalize some values in this way. But this "internalization" is often an example of the second outcome of punishment described earlier, namely blind conformity. There is a great difference between telling the truth to avoid being punished and telling the truth out of the conviction that it is best for human beings to deal honestly with each other. Children do not learn such a principle merely by internalization. Such a principle must be constructed from within, by each individual, over time, through the exchange of points of view with other human beings.

Intellectual Autonomy

In the intellectual realm, too, parents and educators generally assume that children acquire knowledge by internalization from the environment. It is true that we can teach children to say that 7 X 7 = 49, and that a photon is "a quantum of light energy, the energy being proportional to the frequency of the radiation." Schools use grades as a form of reward and punishment to get children to internalize such bits of knowledge.

If a first grader writes 7 + 7 = 13, most teachers put an "X" next to this answer. However, it would be better for the teacher to refrain from responding in this way, and, instead, encourage the child to exchange viewpoints with others. For example, the teacher can ask if everybody else agrees. He or she can also ask the child to prove his answer. Children who are thus encouraged to explain their ideas often correct themselves autonomously. Children ought to be educated to accept ideas only if the ideas make sense. Instead, schools make them recite "right" answers by using grades and smiley faces, from kindergarten to the university.

Piaget built, with 60 years of research, a theory called constructivism. According to this theory, children acquire knowledge by creating one level after another of being "wrong," rather than by internalizing correct, adult knowledge from the beginning. The most obvious example of the constructive process is young children learning to talk. They do not speak in complete sentences from the beginning and do not say, for instance, "Please take an orange down from the shelf and peel it for me." Sinclair (personal communication) gives the example of a child who said, "Want orange," as he pointed to a high shelf. When she gave the orange to him, the child handed it back to her saying, "Open." No one teaches children to say "Want orange" and "Open," but children create their own knowledge out of what they experience in the environment. These "wrong" ideas are necessary steps in children's construction of increasingly higher levels of knowledge.

If children were allowed to construct their own knowledge autonomously by going through one level after another of making

102

sense out of phenomena, there would be far more pupils "turned on" and excited about science, math and every other subject. The role of the teacher should be to get children intrigued about phenomena and to get them engaged in whatever intrigues them (Duckworth, 1987). Instead, schools have traditionally required the memorization of information, and the recent emphasis on standardized achievement test scores are making children (as well as teachers) even more heteronomous.

Autonomy As the Goal of Education

Schools do not intentionally conceptualize heteronomy as their goal. But, by being unaware of autonomy and heteronomy, schools function as if heteronomy were the aim of education. Teachers and principals control children rather than encouraging them to construct from within their own beliefs about what is right in the moral realm and what is true in the intellectual realm.

It may seem more efficient to give ready-made rules and to explain why these rules are necessary. But it is much more effective in the long run to let children experience problems and to ask them what they think they can do about them. Children often come up with the same rules adults would have made, but the difference is that they are more likely to respect the rules they made for themselves. If we encouraged them to make and enforce their own rules during the 10-20 years of schooling, they would become much better able to govern themselves than the majority of adults today.

In the intellectual realm, too, it would be far better for schools not to impose the bits of knowledge that are forgotten shortly after the test. If we encouraged children to be intrigued about things and to make sense critically of what they encounter during the 10-20 years they spend in school, future generations would be far better educated and intelligent than the majority of adults today. Space does not permit me to discuss autonomy adequately, and I urge the reader to refer to Piaget (1932; 1948, Ch. 4), Kamii (1979, 1984, 1985), Fromm (1941), and Milgram (1974) for more examples and explanations.

The tragedy of American education now is that it is on the bandwagon of "quick fixes." Education has traditionally emphasized the memorization of information that did not make much sense to the learner. Things have become worse in recent years because the great majority of educators are on the achievement-test bandwagon.

Teachers and principals worry about test scores, and few stop to ask if the pressure to produce higher scores is good for children's development.

Testmania is a symptom of adult heteronomy. Troubled by newspapers' publication of test scores, school boards all over the country are ordering superintendents to produce scores that are above the national average. Superintendents pass the order down to principals, and principals in turn decree that teachers produce higher test scores. The fact is that, by definition, achievement tests are made so that half of the population necessarily have to be below the national average.

It is time for educators to become more autonomous and to stop being dictated to by politicians, the public and the news media. It is important for educators to become more autonomous because heteronomous adults cannot raise children to become autonomous. The future of education depends not on money and technology, but on our reconceptualizing our goal and reexamining our means.

References

Duckworth, E. (1987). The having of wonderful ideas' and other essays on teaching and learning. New York: Teachers College Press.

Fromm, E. (1941). Escape from freedom. New York: Rinehart & Co.

Kamii, C. (1979). Piaget's theory, behaviorism, and other theories in education. Journal of Education, 161, 13-33.

Kamii, C. (1984). Autonomy: The aim of education envisioned by Piaget. Phi Delta Kappan, 65, 410-415.

Kamii, C. (1985). Young children reinvent arithmetic. New York: Teachers College Press.

Milgram, S. (1974). Obedience to authority New York: Harper & Row.

Piaget, J. (1932). The moral judgment of the child. New York: Free Press, 1965 (translation).

Piaget, J. (1948). To understand is to invent. New York: Viking, 1973 (translation).

SELECTED BIBLIOGRAPHY

Manning, M., Manning, G., & Kamii, C. Early phonics instruction: Its effect on literacy development. Young Children, in press.

Kamii, C. Place value: An explanation of its difficulty and educational implications for the primary grades. Journal of Research in Childhood Education, 1986, 1, 75-86.

Kamii, C. Autonomy vs. heteronomy (comments on "Three preschool curriculum models: Academic and social outcomes" by D. P. Weikart and L. J. Schweinhart). Principal, 1986, 66, 68-70.

Kamii, C. The mental image: A question that remains open. In D. Bergen (Ed.), Play as a learning medium (2nd ed.). Exeter, N. H.: Heinemann, in press.

Bovet, M., Parrat-Dayan, S., & Kamii, C. Early conservation: What Does It Mean? The Journal of Psychology, 1986, 120, 21-35.

Williams, C., & Kamii, C. How do children learn by handling objects? Young Children, 1986, 42, 23-26.

Kamii, C. Cognitive learning and development. In Bernard Spodek (Ed.), Today's Kindergarten. New York: Teachers College Press, 1986.

Kamii, C. Book review of The equilibration of cognitive structures (by Jean Piaget). American Journal of Education, 1986, 94, 574-577.

Kamii, C., Uchiyama, Y., Shimbo, M., Tsuchihashi, H., and Sakano, N. Child care centered on the child. Hoiku Senka (published in Tokyo), 1986, 13, 40-53 (No. 10) and 83-91 (No. 11).

Kamii, C. Leading primary education toward excellence: Beyond worksheets and drill. Young Children, 1985, 40, 3-9. Reprinted in Annual editions: Early childhood education 86/87. Guilford, Conn.: Dushkin Publishing Group, 1986.

Kamii, C., Cesareo, Y., & Mounoud, H. Des Jeux de cartes: La mathematique a 5-8 ans dans une optique piagetienne. Geneva (Switzerland): Faculte de Psychologie et des Sciences de l'Education, Universite de Geneve, 1985 (Cahier de la Section des sciences de l'education No. 41).

Kamii, C. Que aprenen els nens amb la manipulacio dels objectes? In-fan-ci-a (published in Barcelona), 1985, 22, 6-10.

Kamii, C. Evaluation: It all depends on your theory. Australian Journal of Early Education, 1985, 10, 3-9.

Kamii, C., & Randazzo, M. Social interaction and invented spelling. Language Arts, 1985, 62, 124-133.

Manning, M., Manning, G., & Kamii, C. When was 1864? Also: Reading comprehension -- Making it work. Early Years, 1985, 15, 38-40.

Willert, M. K., & Kamii, C. Reading in kindergarten: Direct vs. indirect teaching. Young Children, 1985, 40, 3-9.

Kamii, C. Young children reinvent arithmetic. New York: Teachers College Press, 1985. Translated into Spanish and Portuguese.

Kamii, C. Intellectual and moral autonomy: Operational implications in child development (Resource Materials 16). Paris: UNESCO Unit for Co-Operation with UNICEF & WFP, 1984.

Kamii, C. Comments on "Teachers as learners" by E. Duckworth. The Genetic Epistemologist, 1984, 13 No. 2), 6-8.

Kamii, C. Evaluacion: Todo depende de su teoria. Proceedings of the International Seminar on "Experiences and Alternative Projects in Early Childhood Education" of the World Organization for Preschool Education, Vina del Mar, Chile, August 1-3, 1984.

Kamii, C. The unimportance of Piagetian stages: A note to authors of educational psychology texts. Newsletter of the AERA SIG on Piagetian Theory and Education, Spring, 1984 (Vol. 2, No. 1), 1-3.

Kamii, C. Obedience is not enough. Young Children, 1984, 39, 11-14. Reprinted in : J. Brown McCracken (Ed.), Stress and young children. Washington, D. C.: National Association for the Education of Young Children, in press. Also, Communicator (a publication of the California Association for the Gifted), 1985, 15, 7-9. Translations: The Journal of Nursery Education, 1984, 32, 18-21 (published in Tokyo). In-fan-ci-a, 1983, 13, 19-23 (published in Barcelona). Limen, 1985, Ano 13, No. 89, 8-10 (published in Buenos Aires).

Kamii, C. El concocimiento fisico: Una aplicacion de la teoria de Piaget en preescolar. In Cesar Coll (Ed.), Psicologia genetica y aprendizajes escolares. Madrid: Siglo XXI de Espana, 1983, 57-77.

Kamii, C. Autonomy: The aim of education envisioned by Piaget. Phi Delta Kappan, 1984, 65, 410-415. Abridged and reprinted in Australian Journal of Early Childhood, 1985, 10, 3-10.

Kamii, C. Autonomy as the aim of education. Innovation, 1983 (Numbers 38/39), 8-12 (published in Geneva, Switzerland, by the International Bureau of Education). Translations: Sogo Kyoiku Gijutsu, 1983, 37, 103-115 (published in Tokyo). L'Educateur, 1983 (No. 8), 26-30 (published Cannes, France). Modern Kindergarten, 1983, 10, 23-31(published in Athens). Technique d'Instruction, 1982 (2/82), 29-47 (published in Meyrin, Switzerland).

Kamii, C. L'arithmetique en premiere primaire sans crayons. Math-Ecole, 1983, No. 106, 16-23 (published in Geneva, Switzerland).

Kamii, C. Constructivist education: A direction for the twenty-first century. SEEDBED, 1983, No. 15, 45-65 (published by Teachers' Center Project, Southern Illinios University at Edwardsville).

Kamii, C., Nikai, N., & Tsubota, K. Is primary arithmetic satisfactory? Kyoiku Gijutsu, Grade 1, 1982, 36, 66-72. Also in Kyoiku Gijutsu, Grade 2, 1982, 35, 96-105 (published in Tokyo).

Kamii, C. First graders invent arithmetic: Using Piaget's theory in the classroom. In S. Wagner (Ed.), Proceedings of the Fourth Annual Meeting, North American Chapter, International Group for the Psychology of Mathematics Education. Athens, Georgia: University of Georgia, 1982, 93-99. Reprinted in: G. Abbott Clayton (Ed.), Effective Mathematics Teaching: A Handbook for Classroom Teachers. Tuscaloosa, Alabama: John Seymour SEVCO Press, in press.

Kamii, C. Do schools contribute to mental health? An answer from a Piagetian perspective. Proceedings of the USC-UAP 12th Annual Interdisciplinary International Conference of Piagetian Theory and the Helping Professions, Los Angeles, 1982, in press.

Kamii, C. Encouraging thinking in mathematics. Phi Delta Kappan, 1982, 64, 247-251.

Kamii, C. La autonomia como finalidad de la educacion. Infancia y aprendizaje, 1982, 18 3-32 (published in Madrid). ´

Kamii, C. Do schools contribute to mental health? Academic Psychology Bulletin, 1982, 4, 441-451.

Kamii, C. L'arithmetique en premiere primaire sans crayons. Proceedings of Les primeres jornades sobre nueves perspectives sobre la representacio escrita en el nen, Institut Municipal d'Educacio and Institut de Ciencies de l'Educacion, Universitat de Barcelona, 1982.

Kamii, C. Number in preschool and kindergarten, Washington, D. C.: National Association for the Education of Young Children, 1982.

Kamii, C. La autonomia como finalidad de la educacion. Mexico City: UNICEF (Programa Regional de Estimulacion Temprana), 1982.

Kamii, C. O conhecimento fisico e o numero na escola infantil: Abordagem Piagetiana. Apprentissage/Development, Aprendizaje/Desarrollo, Learning/Development (published in Lisbon), 1981, No. 3, 3 trimestre, 9-28.

Kamii, C. Teachers' autonomy and scientific training. Young Children, 1981, 36, 5-14. Abridged and reprinted in Education Digest, October, 1981.

Kamii, C. Piaget for principals. Principal, 1981, 60, 12-17.

Kamii, C. Application of Piaget's theory to education: The preoperational level. In I. E. Sigel, D. M. Brodzinsky and R. M. Golinkoff (Eds.), New directions in Piagetian theory and practice. Hillsdale, N. J.: Erlbaum Associates, 1981.

Kamii, C. Training teachers to use Piaget's theory in early education. Enfance (published in Paris), 1980, No. special 4/5/1980 (Congres International de Psychologie de l'Enfant, Paris, 1-8 juillet, 1979). 319-20.

Kamii, C. La connaissance physique et le nombre a l'ecole enfantine: Approche piagetiene. Geneva (Switzerland): Faculte de Psychologie et des Sciences de l'Education, Universite de Geneve, 1980 (Cahiers de la Section des sciences de l'education, No. 21).

Kamii, C., & DeVries, R. Group games in early education: Implications of Piaget's theory. Washington, D. C.: National Association for the Education of Young Children, 1980.

Kamii, C. Teaching for thinking and creativity in science education: A Piagetian point of view. In A. E. Lawson (Ed.), The 1979 AETS yearbook: The psychology of teaching for thinking and creativity. Columbus, Ohio: ERIC/SMEAC, 1979.

Kamii, C., & Lee-Katz, L. Physics in preschool education: A Piagetian approach. Young Children, 1979, 34, 4-9. Reprinted in J. R. Brown(Ed.), Curriculum planning for young children. Washington, D. C.: National Association for the Education of Young Children, 1982, 171-176.

Kamii, C. Piaget's theory, behaviorism, and other theories in education. Journal of Education, 1979, 161, 13-33.

Kamii, C., & DeVries, R. Physical knowledge in preschool education: Implications of Piaget's theory. Englewood Cliffs, N.J.: Prentice-Hall, 1978.

Kamii, C., & DeVries, R. Piaget for early education. In M. C. Day & R. K. Parker (Eds.), The preschool in action (2nd ed.). Boston: Allyn and Bacon, 1977.

Kamii, C. & Derman, L. The Engelmann approach to teaching logical thinking: Findings from the administration of some Piagetian tasks. In D. R. Green, M.P. Ford, & G. B. Flamer (Eds.), Measurement and Piaget. New York: McGraw-Hill, 1971.

Kamii, C. K., & Radin, N. L. Class differences in the socialization practices of Negro mothers. Journal of Marriage and the Family, 1967, 29, 302-310. (Reprinted in R. E. Staples (Ed.), The black family: Essays and studies. Belmont, Calif.: McCutchan, 1970, pp. 189-195.

Lilian G. Katz

AUTOBIOGRAPHICAL SKETCH OF
LILIAN G. KATZ

Professor of Early Childhood Education; Director, ERIC Clearinghouse on Elementary and Early Childhood Education, University of Illinois, Urbana-Champaign.

Editor-in-Chief: Early Childhood Research Quarterly; Vice President, National Association for the Education of Young Children.

Personal History:
Born: London, England, 1932; immigrated to U.S., 1947; married Boris Katz, 1952; naturalized U.S. citizen 1953; two sons (Daniel, b. 1954 and Stephen, b. 1956), one daughter (Miriam, b. 1957).

Educational Background:
1943-47   Burlington School for Girls; Trinity College of Music, London, England
1950 Graduated from Woodrow Wilson High School, Los Angeles, California
1950-1954 Undergraduate: Whittier College, California (2 years); San Francisco State College (Modern Languages) (2 years)
1954-1962 Full Time Child Rearing
1957-1962 Participating Mother in Parent Cooperative Nursery Schools, San Francisco Bay Area
1964   B.A. Cum Laude, San Francisco State College (Social Sciences)
1964-1968 Stanford University, School of Education: 1964-66, Research Assistant, Lab. for Human Development; 1966-67, U.S.O.E. Research Training Fellow; 1968, Ph.D. Psychological Studies (Ch. Development)

Professional Background:
California:
1962-1964 Teacher: Redwood Parents' Nursery School and Parent Educator for Sequoia Adult School, Redwood City, California
1965(sum.) Demonstration Teacher: Harold E. Jones Child Study Center Nursery School

University of Illinois (Urbana-Champaign):
1968-1970   Asst. Prof. of Early Childhood Education
1970-1973   Assoc. Prof. of Early Childhood Education
1973-pres.   Prof. of Early Childhood Education
1970-pres.   Director, ERIC Clearinghouse on Elementary and Early Childhood Education
1979-1981   Chairman, Dept. of Elementary and Early Childhood Education
1979-1982   Co-Director, Research Unit on Teacher Education

Visiting Professorships:
Foreign:
1975   Schoolmaster's Fellow, College of St. Matthias, Bristol, England Scholar in Residence)
1976   Visiting Professor of Education, Macquarie University, Sydney, Australia
            Visiting Lecturer, St. Mary's College, Cheltenham, Gloucestershire, England
1981   Visiting Professor, University of Hamburg, West Germany
1983   Visiting Professor, University of Baroda, India (Fulbright)
            Visiting Professor, University of the West Indies (Cave Hill Campus, Barbados)
1984   University of British Columbia, Vancouver, British Columbia, Canada (short course)
            Visiting Lecturer, Beijing Normal University, China (Short course)

U.S.: (short courses)
San Francisco State College
Texas Women's University
University of Wisconsin-Stout
University of Utah
Hawaii Loa College
University of Northern Iowa
Minot State University, Minot, North Dakota

Special Honors and Appointments, etc:
1969   Named Outstanding Woman Doctoral Graduate, School of Education, 1968, Stanford University, Stanford, California

1970-1971   President, Illinois Association for the Education of Young Children
1969-1971   Editorial Advisory Board, National Association for the Education of Young Children
1973   Named as one of 27 "Scholars of Excellence" of the University of Illinois
1974   UNESCO Consultant, Training Mission, Barbados, W.I.
1975   Public Representative, CDA Consortium Board
1980   President, United States National Committee of OMEP(Organisation Mondiale pour l'Education Prescholaire)
1980-1982   Chairman, National Task Force for Child Development Associate
1980-1986   Chairman: Pre-primary Project, International Evaluation Association
1980-1982   Consulting Editor for all Early Childhood Entries in Encyclopedia of Educational Research, Fifth Edition, AERA, Macmillan, 1982
1981-pres. Editorial Board, Children in Contemporary Society
1982   Elected Fellow of Division 7: American Psychological Association
1983   Fulbright Fellow: University of Baroda, India
1985   Elected Fellow of Division 15: American Psychological Association
1985   Chairman, Education Committee, Council for International Exchange of Scholars (Fulbright)
            Advisory Board - Learning Magazine
            William and Sarah Hewett Summer Award for International Studies
1986   National Advisory Board - Lipman School and Research Center, Memphis State University, Tenn.

BASIC NEEDS OF YOUNG CHILDREN

The question of what young chldren "need" for healthy development is a complex one. Aside from such basics as food, water, air, shelter and affection, most other so-called basic needs are learned. These needs cannot be determined empirically (Dearden, 1972). In this sense, needs are culture-bound. My view of the basic needs of young children are set out below in terms of seven related propositions.

1. The young child needs an optimum feeling of safety.

This proposition refers to psychological safety, usually referred to as feeling secure, connected and attached to one or more others. Children's feelings of attachment derive from perceiving that what they do or feel really matters to others: matters enough that they will pick them up, comfort them, get angry and even scold them, as well as take pleasure in their company, their growth and triumphs. The opposite of attachment is indifference.

Experiencing oneself as attached, connected or safe, comes not just from being loved, but from feeling loved, feeling wanted, feeling significant, etc., to an optimum (not maximum) degree. Note that the emphasis is more on feeling loved and wanted than on being loved and wanted. It is unlikely that children feel loved if in fact they are not; but it is possible for children to be loved by someone without being able to feel it. While it is clear that children need to feel loved, they thrive best then they feel loved by someone they can look up to.

2. Young children need adults who accept the authority that is theirs by virtue of their greater experience, knowledge and wisdom.

This proposition is based on the assumption that neither parents nor educators are caught between the extremes of authoritarianism or permissiveness. Authoritarianism can be described as the exercise of power without warmth, encouragement or explanation. Permissiveness is the abdication of power, though it provides warmth, encouragement and support to children. Rather than either of these extremes, children need adults who are authoritative, i.e., who exercise their very considerable power over the lives of young children accompanied by warmth, support, encouragement and adequate explanations. The concept of authoritativeness also includes treating children with respect, i.e., treating their opinions, feelings, wishes and ideas as valid even when we disagree with them. To respect people we agree with is no great problem; respecting those whose ideas, wishes, and feelings are different from ours may be a mark of wisdom in parents and genuine professionalism in teachers.

3. Every child needs optimum self-esteem.

Self-esteem is developed through interaction with significant others: adults, siblings and peers, throughout the growing years. It is not acquired on a particular day to last forever. It fluctuates with the vicissitudes of daily life. Self-esteem is strengthened when children are engaged in challenging activities and not from quick and cheap success experiences. Just because criticism undermines self-esteem, flattery does not build it.

One cannot have self-esteem in a vacuum. Our self-esteem results from evaluations of ourselves against criteria acquired early in life from families, neighborhoods, ethnic groups and later on from peer groups and the larger community. The criteria against which we assess how acceptable and worthy we are vary somewhat from one family, one neighborhood, one ethnic group to another. In some families beauty is criterion; in others, neatness or athletic ability or toughness are important criteria of acceptability.

Educators have to be sensitive to the self-esteem criteria children bring to school with them. The family's definition of the "good boy" or the "good girl," may be different from the school's. A teacher's disrespect or violation of the self-esteem criteria that children bring from home is unwise, since all children need to be able to respect their own families.

4. Every child needs to experience life as worth living, reasonably satisfying, interesting and authentic.

This proposition suggests that we involve children in activities and interactions, which are real to them, significant to them and that engage their minds. Children do not need to be amused, titilated or treated like pets with gnomelike creatures smiling down on them from every classroom wall. The widespread Disneyesque decor, the classroom environments that are superficial, phony, shallow, fanciful and trivial threaten children's intellects. It suggests also that we resist the temptation to settle just for what amuses them. The real and natural world is full of events and phenomena young children find intriguing; it does not need to be dolled up with gnomes, fairies and talking animals.

5. Children need help from others to make sense of their experiences.

A major responsibility of adults is to help children improve, extend, refine and deepen their own understandings of their worlds. As they grow older they need help with their understandings of other peoples' worlds. It is assumed that children's learning proceeds from first-hand direct experience to second-hand indirect experience. Therefore, the education that we provide for young children should be oriented to helping them make fuller and better sense of their first-hand experiences.

6. Young children need optimum association with adults and older children who exemplify the personal qualities we want them to acquire.

Although there may be some variations among us, it is likely that we agree on many qualities we want all children to acquire, e.g., the capacity to care for and about others, honesty, kindness, acceptance of those who are different from themselves, the love of learning and so forth.

This proposition suggests that we look around the children's environments and ask: To what extent do our children have contact with people who exhibit these qualities? Or, on the other hand, to what extent do our children observe people who are attractive and glamorous but do not have the qualities we want them to develop? It seems to me that children need communities and societies that take the necessary steps to protect them from excessive exposure to violence and crime and other distortions of personality during the the early years while their characters are still in formation.

7. Children need relationships with adults who are willing to take a stand on what is worth doing, worth having, worth knowing and worth caring about.

This proposition seems to belabor the obvious. But in an age of increasing and justifiable concern about pluralism, multiculturalism and community participation, professionals are often hesitant and apologetic about their own values. It seems to me that such hesitancy in taking stands on what is worthwhile causes us to give our children mixed signals about what is expected and what is worth knowing and doing. When we do take a stand, it does not guarantee that our children will accept or agree with our version of the "good life." We must, in fact, cultivate our capacities to respect alternative definitions of the worthwhile life. Taking a stand with quiet conviction and courage may help the young to more easily see us as thinking and caring individuals who have enough self-respect to respect our own values as well as the values of others.

REFERENCES

Dearden, R. F. (1972) "Needs" in education. In R. F. Dearden, P. H. Hirst, R. S. Peters (Eds.) Education and the Development of Reason. London: Routledge Kegan Paul.

SELECTED BIBLIOGRAPHY

JOURNALS:

"Follow-up Studies: Are They Worth the Trouble?" Journal of Teacher Education, 32 (2) March-April, 1981, 18-24 (with J. Raths, et al.).

"The Best of Intentions for the Education of Teachers." (with J. D. Raths), Action in Teacher Education, Spring, 1982.

"Advice for Inservice Education on Helping Teachers," Educational Perspectives, XX, Summer, 1981, 16-21 and The Education Digest, February, 1982.

"Perspectives on Mothering and Teaching," Australian Journal of Early Childhood Education, 7 (1), March, 1982, pp.4-15.

"Child and Family. Demographic Develoments in the OCED Countries. A Review." CERI, OECD. In International Review Education, 28 (1), 1982, 126-127.

"Planning Programs for Young Children: What Should Early Childhood Education Be About?" World Book-Childcraft. Resource Report. 1983.

"Distinction entre maternage et eduation." Revue des sciences de l'education, 9 (2), 1983, 301-19.

"Professional Judgement in Preschool Teaching," Views, 10 (1), Fall, 1983, 4-16.

"Notes on Staff Communications," Review 1984, Cleveland Association for the Education of Young Children, 1984, 4-9.

"The Professional Early Childhood Teacher," Young Children, 39 (5), July 1984, 3-10.

"Some Issues in the Dissimination of Child Development Knowledge," Newsletter, Society for Child Development, Fall, 1984, 7-9.

"Fostering Communicative Competence in Young Children." In Margaret M. Clark (ED.), Helping Communication in Early Education. Educational Review, Birmingham, England, United Kingdom, 1985.

"Current Perspectives on Child Development" Bulletin of the Council for Research in Music Education; Bulletin No. 86, Winter 1986, 1-9.

"Dispositions as Goals for Teacher Education." (with James D. Raths). Teaching and Teacher Education, Vol. 1, No. 4, pp. 301-307, 1985.

"Research Currents: Teachers as Learners." Language Arts, 62 (7), November, 1985, 778-82.

"Framework for Research on Teacher Education Programs." Journal of Teacher Education (36) 6 Nov.-Dec. 9-15.

"Preventing School Failure: The Relationship Between Preschool and Primary Education" A Review. International Review of Education (32), 4, 489-450.

CHAPTERS:

"Problems and Issues in Teacher Education," B. Spodek (ED.), Teacher Education. National Association for the Education of Young Children, Washington, D.C., 1974.

"The Socialization of Teachers for Early Childhood Education," B. Spodek and H. Walberg (Eds.), Early Childhood Education. National Society for the Study of Education, Chicago, McCutchan, 1977.

"The Role of Ideology in the Education of Young Children," and "Guidelines for Teachers," J. Oremland (Ed.), Sexual and Gender Development. Cambridge, Mass: Ballinger Press. 1977. 285-292.

"Some Generic Principles of Teaching," K. Devaney (Ed.), Essays on Teachers' Centers, Far West Lab. on Ed. Res., San Francisco, Calif., 1977.

"Professional Ethics in Early Childhood Education," S. Kilmer (ed.), Advances in Early Education and Day Care, Vol. 1, 1979.

"Mothering and Teaching: Significant Distinctions." In L. Katz (ed.), Current Topics in Early Childhood Education, Vol. 3, Ablex Publishing Corp., 1980.

"Contemporary Perspectives on the Roles of Mothers and Teachers." In Parenthood in a Changing Society, ERIC/EECE, University of Illinois, 1980.

"Ethical Issues in Working with Young Children." In D. T. Streets (Ed.) Administering Day Care and Preschool Programs. Allyn & Bacon, Boston, Massachusetts, I982.

"Early Childhood Education," Husen and Postelthwaite, (Eds.), International Encyclopedia of Education: Research and Studies. Pergammon Press. London, England, U.K., 1985.

"Teacher Education for Early Childhood Education," Husen & Postelthwaite (Eds.), International Encyclopedia of Education: Research and Studies. Pergammon Press. London, England, U.K., 1985.

"The Education of Preprimary Teachers." In L. Katz, (Ed.), Current Topics in Early Childhood Education, Vol. 5, Ablex Publishing Corp., 1984.

"Professional Relationships in Child Care." In T. Philpot (Ed.), Group Care Practice: The Challenge of the Next Decade. Business Press International, Surrey, England, United Kingdom, 1984.

"Teacher Education for Early Childhood Education." In M. Dunkin (Ed.) International Encyclopedia of Teaching and Teacher Education. London: Pergammon. 1986.

"Un cadre structurel pour recherches sur la formation des enseignants" (with J. D. Raths). In M. Crahay and D. Lafontaine, (Eds.) L'Art et la Science de L. Enseignement Leige, Belgium: Editions Labor. pp. 387-410.

"The Nature of Professions: Where is Early Childhood Education?" In B. Spodek, D. Peters and O. Saracho (Eds.) Professionalism and Early Childhood Education, Teachers' College Press. In press.

Also in:

P. Heaslip, (Ed.) The Challenge of the Future, (Professional Issues in Early Childhood Education). Bristol Polytechnic: Bristol, England. 1986. 5-27.

"Issues in the Preparation of Teachers of Young Children." In B. Day (Ed.) Perspectives on Early Childhood Education. North Carolina Press. In press.

"Early Education: What Should Young Children Be Doing?" in L. Kagan & E. Zigler Early Schooling: The National Debate. New Haven: Yale University Press. In press.

BOOKS EDITED:

Current Research and Perspectives in Open Education: A Research Review from EKNE. D. Dwain Hern, Joel Burdin and Lillian G. Katz (Eds.). American Association of Elementary, Kindergarten and Nursery Eductors (EKNE), Washington, D.C., 1973, 173p.

Current Topics in Early Childhood Education. (Editor-in-Chief), Vol.I, Ablex Publishing Corp., Norwood, N.J., 1977.

Current Topics in Early Childhood Education. (Editor-in-Chief), Vol. II, Ablex Publishing Corp., Norwood, N.J., 1979.

Current Topics in Early Childhood Education. (Editor-in-Chief), Vol. III, Ablex Publishing Corp., Norwood, N.J., 1980.

Current Topics in Early Childhood Education.(Editor-in-Chief), Vol. IV, Ablex Publishing Corp., Norwood, N.J., 1982.

Current Topics in Early Childhood Education. (Editor-in-Chief), Vol. V, Ablex Publishing Corp., Norwood, N.J., 1984.

Advances in Teacher Education, Vol. I, (Co-editor with J. D. Raths), Ablex Publishing Corp., Norwood, N.J., 1984.

Advances in Teacher Education, Vol. II, (Co-editor with J. D. Raths), Norwood, N.J., Ablex Publishing Corp., l986.

Current Topics in Early Childhood Education, Vol. VI. Norwood, N.J., Ablex Publishing Corp., 1986.

Current Topics in Early Childhood Education, Vol. VII. Norwood, N.J., Ablex Publishing Corp. In press.

BOOKS:

Talks with Teachers: Reflections on Early Childhood Education. National Association for the Education of Young Children, Washington, D.C., 1977. 117p. (Translated into Chinese.)

Talks with Parents: On Living with Preschoolers. ERIC/EECE, University of Illinois, Urbana, Ill., 1983.

More Talks with Teachers. ERIC/EECE, University of Illinois, Urbana, Ill., 1984. (Translated into Chinese.)

Professionalism, Child Development and Dissemination: Three Topics. Urbana, Ill. ERIC Clearinghouse on Elementary and Early Childhood Education. 1986.

COLUMNS:

Parents Magazine, Monthly column, "As They Grow: 3/4 (year olds)", since November, 1978 until present.

Instructor, Monthly column, "Ask Dr. Katz," 1983-1984.

Linda Leonard Lamme

AUTOBIOGRAPHICAL SKETCH OF
LINDA LEONARD LAMME

I grew up in Babylon, Long Island, and attended Principia College, the University of Illinois, and Syracuse University (Ph.D., 1974). My first public school teaching job was a fourth grade in Fisher, Illinois. The class was diverse: Mennonite children, farm children, and Air Force children. Some of the children read adult novels and some could not read. What I remember most fondly was the cloak room and the children lining the walls with jars of flowers (dandelions) in the spring. I taught sixth grade for three years in Fayetteville, New York, and for one year in Brazil, Indiana. In Brazil, the children and I walked to the public library once a week because the school did not have a library. We published a newspaper called the "Meridian Monitor." It was my best year of teaching.

A close friend of my father-in-law once asked me, on the year that he retired, "What do schools do that make some people, like myself, avid readers, while others, who can read equally, never pick up a book?" This "uncle" never travelled anywhere without something to read. He even shipped ahead a crate of books when he spent six weeks on a South Pacific Island. He is spending an active, enjoyable retirement, doing a lot of what he loves best -- reading. His question spurred my interest in children's reading habits.

At Syracuse, I studied with Margaret Early and Margaret Lay-Dopyera. Both were outstanding scholars and teachers. I also taught 12 hours a semester -- courses in language arts, early childhood education, and children's literature -- and supervised student teachers. My dissertation was a study of the relationships between children's reading abilities and their reading habits.

I've been at the University of Florida since 1974. Ira Gordon had a practice of writing new professors into his grants, so I credit his generosity and leadership with getting me off to the right start in conducting research and writing. I was hired to teach language arts, reading, and children's literature in an early childhood program. Those subjects remain my areas of interest and expertise.

I couldn't close an autobiographical statement without sharing how much my own children, Laurel Agnes, now 10, and Ary, now 2, have taught me about emergent literacy. My two most recent books, Growing Up Writing and Growing Up Reading are based upon my experiences with my own children. My supportive husband has helped me become a better writer.

REFLECTIONS ON RAISING LITERATE CHILDREN

I believe that parents are children's first and most important teachers. Ira Gordon maintained that if schools did not work with parents, they were merely perpetuating the status quo. Children's learning begins before birth. Parents need to understand the importance of spending time with their babies reading, singing, and writing with them so that they grow up reading and writing. It is a national tragedy that day care is necessary for so many of our children so early in life. Until kindergarten, the best place for young children is at home with half-day nursery school socialization experiences. If our government cared for children, we would make it possible for families to survive economically with many more part-time and job sharing opportunities for families with young children. Women or men who take time to stay at home with their babies should not suffer employment penalties and should be subsidized by our government. Raising children is parents' most important work.

Our goals for literacy instruction need to be that children learn to love to read and write. For children who love to read and write will read and write, and children who do read and write become competent readers and writers. The reverse is not true. Too many of our schools have very limited goals -- teaching children how to read and write. A person who can read, but does not, is no better off than a person who cannot read. Most of what goes on in school -- worksheets, skillpacks, round robin reading, spelling tests, copying from the board, grades -- does not promote a love of literacy in young children.

Our school classrooms need to be made more like our most literate homes. Basic skills approaches to literacy are developmentally inappropriate for kindergarten and the primary grades. Whole language methods in reading involve lap reading, reading aloud to children, storytelling, story enactment, and sustained silent reading. Children read high quality children's books, and children's literature. Reading groups are heterogeneous in ability. Children reading similar types of books form groups and participate in projects eminating from their reading. They discuss comprehension questions. The focus throughout reading instruction is on meaning and communication, not on decoding.

Children can write long before they can spell conventionally. Developmentally appropriate instruction encourages children to write for communication in kindergarten and the primary grades. Whole language classrooms have mailboxes, children's writing displayed on low walls, and a writing center stocked with stationery, markers, pencils, and paper of various sizes, shapes, textures, and colors. Children write greeting cards, notes, messages, signs, labels, and stories. They keep dialog jounals for personal communication with their teachers. They participate in a writing workshop where they write drafts and try them out in an "author's chair" to get the help and suport of their peers. Teachers publish children's refined writings. Spelling and handwriting are studied after children have become fluent writers, and then, as a part of the proofreading process of writing to communicate, not from basal textbooks.

Adults need to celebrate what children know instead of criticizing what they don't know. For example, parents and teachers can look at the content of what children write and comment upon that rather than grade or correct the spelling and handwriting. We need to encourage beginning readers by taking turns reading with them and supporting their guesses at unfamiliar words rather than correcting their reading errors. Generally, we are supportive of children's block constructions and drawings, yet we criticize their fledgling efforts to read and write. Children don't learn by correction. They have a hard time learning when their self-confidence is low. You build children's self-esteem when you celebrate what they know.

The best instruction for parents or teachers is responsive instruction. Observe children carefully to determine what they are ready to learn and then provide them with the experiences they need to promote that learning. We need to resist the impulse to tell children things, but instead set the stage so they can discover things on their own.

Teachers need to spend as close to 100 per cent of their time teaching as possible. The best teaching is one-to-one or one-to-small group discussion with children. Grading and testing waste the time of both teachers and children. Observational notes and children's productions are all the evidence parents need that their children are learning.

Most elementary school teachers today are not readers and writers themselves. Would a parent let a child take piano lessons from a teacher who did not play the piano? Teachers need to learn how to love to read and write before they can help children become avid readers and writers. A good way for teachers to become readers is to read large quantities of children's literature. Some of the best books being published today are children's books. One way to get hooked on writing is to keep a journal of teaching experiences.

Education's greatest enemy is the television. It is far more addictive than smoking and just as detrimental to one's health and human relations. Preschool children should never watch television. There is always something better to do -- drawing, playing with toys, or playing outside, if not spending time with parents and friends. Preschoolers who watch TV have shorter attention spans and more violent behavior than their non-TV watching peers. The values inculcated on television are detrimental for children of all ages and adults as well -- sensationalism, materialism, violence -- all appeal to our baser instincts. If elementary school children watch television, it should be public television and should be viewed and discussed with parents. The commercials on TV are damaging enough to warrant excluding anything on those channels from children's viewing. Television is mesmeric and addictive. Each time children watch a program it should be well-planned, not the spontaneous viewing of a show that just happens to be on. (Parenthetically, TV is no better for adults. In fact, many senior citizens spend the last years of their lives vegetating and atrophying in front of the TV set.)

The rewards of good teaching aren't monetary. They come from the heartfelt satisfaction of devoting your life to helping others. The close friendships that emerge from genuine relationships in a class where there is confidentiality and good feelings, where teachers and children help and suport each other, are true satisfactions. When teachers take the time to treat each child as though he or she is special, to really get to know children and to communicate with them in meaningful ways, children are happy in school and learn easily. Close, long-lasting ties are formed. I still write to some of the children I taught in elementary school over 20 years ago. Teaching is a marvelously satisfying career, and we need to attract our brightest, most talented, and most sensitive young people into the field.

PUBLICATION BIBLIOGRAPHY

BOOKS:

Lamme, L. Raising Readers: A Guide to Sharing Literature with Young Children. (with J. Matanzo, M. Olson, and V. Cox) New York: Walker and Company, 1980.

Lamme, L. (Ed.) Learning to Love Literature. Urbana, IL: National Council of Teachers of English, 1981.

Lamme, L. Growing Up Writing. Washington, D.C.: Acropolis Books, 1984.

Lamme, L. Growing Up Reading. Washington, D.C.: Acropolis Books, 1985.

CHAPTERS:

Lamme, L. "Children's Literature: The Natural Way to Learn to Read," in Cullinan, B. (Ed.), Children's Literature in the Reading Program. Newark, Delaware: International Reading Association, 1987.

REFEREED PUBLICATIONS:

Lamme, A. and Lamme, L. "Utilizing the Earth's Grid," Journal of Geography, 66 (November, 1967): 425-427.

Lamme, A. and Lamme, L. "Prediction in Geography," Journal of Geography, 68 (March, 1969): 155-158.

Lamme, L. "Self-Contained to Departmentalized: How Reading Habits Changed," The Elementary School Journal, 76 (January, 1976): 208-218.

Lamme, L. "Are Reading Habits and Abilities Related?" The Reading Teacher, 30 (October, 1976): 21-27. Reprinted in the William S. Gray Research Collection in Reading.

Lamme, L. "Reading Aloud to Young Children," Language Arts, 53 (November/December, 1976): 886-888.

Lamme, L. and Kane, F. "Children, Books, and Collage," Language Arts, 53 (November/December, 1976): 902-905.

Lamme, L. and Holst, L. "Dialects and Poetry," The Florida English Journal, 2 (July, 1977): 29-32.

Lamme, L. and Olmsted, P. "Family Reading Habits and Children's Progress in Reading," Resources in Education, October, 1977.

Lamme, L. and Ayris, B. "Handwriting in Florida's Public Schools, Florida Journal of Educational Research, 20 (1978): 65-79.

Omotoso, S., and Lamme, L. "Using Wordless Picture Books to Assess Cross-Cultural Differences in Seven Year Olds," The Reading Teacher, 32 (January, 1979): 414-416. Reprinted in the William S. Gray Research Collection in Reading.

Lamme, L. "Song Picture Books -- A Maturing Genre of Children's Literature," Language Arts, 56 (April, 1979): 400-407.

Lamme, L. "Handwriting in an Early Childhood Curriculum," Young Children, 25(November, 1979): 20-27. Reprinted in: Barbe, W. et al., Basic Skills in Kindergarten, Columbus, Ohio: Zaner-Bloser, 1000; Brown, J. (Ed.), Curriculum Planning for Young Children, Washington, D.C.: NAEYC, 1982; Barbe, W., Handwriting: Basic Skills for Effective Communication, Columbus, Ohio: Zaner-Bloser, 1984.

Lamme, L. and Lamme, A. J. "Patterns of Children's Play," Journal of Leisure Research, 11 (Winter, 1979): 253-270.

Lamme, L. "Reading Aloud to Infants," Childhood Education, 56 (April/May, 1980): 285-290. Reprinted as a pamphlet six times. Reprinted in Barron, P. and Burley, J. Jump Over the Moon. New York: Holt, Rinehart & Winston, 1984.

Lamme, A. and Lamme, L. "Children's Food Preferences," Journal of School Health, 50 (September, 1980): 397-402. Revised and reprinted in New York Folklore 5 (November, 1981): 189-196.

Lamme, L. and Denny, P. "A Writing Curriculum for Preschoolers," Day Care and Early Education, (Fall, 1981): 12-15.

Crocker, L., Lamme, L., and Ondresik, T. "Relationship between Children's Writing Performance and Standardized Test Scores," Florida Journal of Educational Research, 23 (1981): 92-98.

Lamme, L. and Ross, D. "Graduate Methods Classes: Do They Influence Teaching Methods?" Journal of Teacher Education, 32 (November/December, 1981): 25-29.

Krogh, S. and Lamme, L. "How Literature Can Help Young Children Learn to Share," Childhood Education, 59 (January/February, 1983): 188-192.

Lamme, L. and Childers, N. "The Composing Processes of Three Young Children," Research in the Teaching of English, 17 (February, 1983): 31-50.

Lamme, L., McMillin M., and Clark, B. "Early Childhood Teacher Certification: A National Survey," Journal of Teacher Education, 34 (March/April, 1983): 44-47.

Lamme, L. "Teaching Handwriting in an Integrated Language Arts Program," Handwriting: Basic Skills for Effective Communication, edited by W. Barbe, V. Lucas, and T. Wasylyk, Columbus, Ohio: Zaner-Bloser, 1984: 202-216.

Lamme, L., and Ayris, B. "Is the Handwriting of Beginning Writers Influenced by Writing Tools?" Journal of Research and Development in Education, 17 (Fall, 1983): 32-38.

Lamme, L. "The Portrayal of Teachers in Books for Children: Teachers in Picture Books, "Proceedings of the "Invincible Louisa Conference, Syracuse University School of Education, (May, 1984): 89-106.

Ross, D. and Lamme, L. "When You Close the Door, the Decisions Are All Yours," Journal of Language Experience, 6 (Summer, 1984): 31-38.

Krogh, S. and Lamme, L. "What About Sharing?--Children's Literature and Moral Development," Young Children, 40 (May, 1985): 48-51. Reprinted in Curriculum Planning: A New Approach by G. Haas (Allyn & Bacon, 1986). Reprinted in Stress and Young Children, edited by J. B. McCracken (NAEYC, 1986).

Lamme, L. "Ten Teachers I'd Like to Meet," Bulletin of the Children's Literature Assembly, 11 (Winter, 1985): 3-4.

Lamme, L. and Tway, E. "Humanistic Teachers in Children's Books," Journal of Humanistic Education, 9 (Spring, 1985): 8-11.

Lamme, L. and Krogh, S. "Distributive Justice and the Moral Development Curriculum," Social Education, 49 (October, 1985): 616-621.

Lamme, L. and Packer, A. "Bookreading Behaviors of Infants," The Reading Teacher, 39 (February, 1986): 504-509.

Lamme, L. "Can All Children Learn How to Read As Early Readers Did?" The Missouri Reader, (Fall, 1986): 2-5.

Shirley C. Raines

AUTOBIOGRAPHICAL SKETCH OF
SHIRLEY C. RAINES

Dr. Shirley C. Raines is an associate professor in Education, Curriculum and Instruction, at George Mason University in Fairfax, Virginia. She teaches courses in language development and curriculum development. Her present research project focuses on young children's responses to wordless picture books.

Shirley graduated from the University of Tennessee in Knoxville with an Ed.D. in Education, Curriculum and Instruction. Her Masters Degree is in Child Development from the University of Tennessee. She also studied child development for her Bachelors Degree in Home Economics Education from the University of Tennessee at Martin.

Before coming to George Mason in 1987, Dr. Raines was the Department Head of Curriculum and Instruction at Northeastern State University in Tahlequah, Oklahoma. In Oklahoma, she worked with Cherokee Nation projects for young children and also developed the Masters Degree in Early Childhood Education. Other university positions included an associate professor at North Carolina Wesleyan, and she also taught at the University of Alabama. While in Alabama, Dr. Raines also chaired the Department of Elementary and Early Childhood Education for one year. During her appointment at the University of Alabama, Shirley taught in the international studies program in Mexico, Colombia, and Ecuador.

Formerly, Shirley was a classroom teacher in Kentucky and Indiana and a Head Start and Title XX Child Care Services Director in Tennessee. She credits her work in staff development in Head Start and a graduate teaching practicum in England as her incentives to enter teacher education.

Her major professor at the University of Tennessee, Knoxville, was Dr. Robert S. Thurman, who encouraged her work in a mentoring role to learn more about the history of teacher education in the early childhood field. Shirley credits Dr. Lynn Cagle and Dr. Lester Knight, also of the University of Tennessee, for her keen interests in Piaget and in children's language development.

Dr. Raines presently is on the governing board of the National Association of Early Childhood Teacher Educators as the treasurer. She also serves on the publications committee for ACEI, the

Association for Childhood Education International, and edits the "Professional Books Column" for <u>Childhood Education</u>. For three years, she edited <u>Oklahoma Children</u> for the Oklahoma Association on Children Under Six. She also is a former State President of Oklahoma ACEI, and in 1987, she received the Association for Childhood Education International Members Recognition Award.

Shirley's expertise in curriculum development, professionalism, and children's language development has resulted in publications in <u>Young Children</u>, <u>Childhood Education</u>, <u>The Reading Teacher</u>, <u>Educational Leadership</u>, and <u>Annual Editions in Early Childhood Education</u>. She edited a book, <u>The Wesleyan Papers: Keeping the Child in Childhood</u>, and wrote a book for R. & E. Research Associates, <u>A Guide to Early Learning</u>. She presently is developing a book for early childhood practitioners on language development.

THREE KEYS TO PROFESSIONALISM
FOR EARLY CHILDHOOD EDUCATORS

One night a center director was returning home late from a parent meeting. As she approached her apartment building, she saw her neighbor crawling around the base of a street light. The neighbor had lost her key and was looking for it. After considerable time and no success with the two of them searching, the director asked, "Are you sure you lost your key here by the street light?" "Well no," replied the neighbor. "I think I dropped it over there in the dark, but I'm looking over here first, 'cause it's easier to see in the light."

This story was adapted from one by Peter Mosenthal (1986). As early childhood professionals, we are like the center director returning home late. We have built programs, trained staff, led policy and legislative initiatives, taught courses, conducted research, revised curricula. We deserve to rest, to take our key, open the door to the apartment and go inside, ignoring the neighbor searching for her lost key. But, we can not.

As early childhood educators, we are professionals who assist others in their searches for their lost keys. We may need to help our colleagues find their lost keys by collaborating on a training project, by sharing a body of information we have uncovered, or by simply cheering them on and supporting them in their searches. The key to professionalism is not just the key we hold in our own hands but the keys our colleagues hold and search for as well.

It is easy to laugh at the neighbor in our story who is crawling around the street light looking for her key, until we remember all the times we have lost our keys and the strange places we found ourselves searching, as looking in a winter coat pocket in the middle of the summer. We often search high and low for lost keys, only to find them in the most obvious place. There are times when it seems we have forgotten the obvious place to look for our professionalism key - in our commitment to quality education and services for children and their families.

Our teaching, our public policy efforts, and the multiplicity of our enduring programs for children and families speaks well for us as a profession. We have a history of commitment to children which transcends the decades and the continents. We have a TRADITION of COMMITMENT. If one were to describe physically what a key looks like which represents a "tradition of commitment," it would be an ornate, old, beautifully crafted, heavy brass key. The weight of which is always apparent in one's hand.

But there are literally thousands of people entering our profession as services and education expand rapidly. They do not know of our history, our story of the profession and do not feel the responsibilities to our traditions of commitment. Part of the enculturation of new students studying the field, of new employees, and of new service givers needs to include the beauty and the weight of the old brass key, our "tradition of commitment." Recognizing the present quality of our endeavors is dependent upon the connection to our history and how we arrived at the standards of quality to which we cling. The beautiful old key representing our "tradition of commitment" was passed on to us by the dauntless women and men who struggled to interpret into sound programs their beliefs about children and about growth and development. We must pass their key on to the new arrivals to the profession to help them unlock the doors to understanding what we do in this profession and why we do what we do. We early childhood professionals who hold the key would scarcely be foolish enough to drop it, for it is heavy and beautiful in our hands.

One of my mentors, Dr. Robert S. Thurman at the University of Tennessee, passed the key onto me when he had me dig through the old manuscripts to read and quote Francis Parker, Patty Smith Hill,

John Dewey, and Elizabeth Peabody. As I read and understood, I felt connected to at least one part of the story of our profession and saw the beautifully crafted key.

But then, keys are changing. There are plastic keys now, nothing more than small rectangles of plastic with holes punched into them. Slip one into your hotel room door, the lock clicks and the door opens. The punched holes contain the combination. When you finish your stay, you throw the key away. Another combination is placed in the computer for the next person and another key is punched.

Plastic disposable keys represent innovations, the new and changing, but plastic keys with the right combinations are successful in opening locked doors. Shall we disdain the use of the plastic key because it is new and so different from the weighty old brass one? No, if the plastic key is an innovation with the right combination punched in, we will use it, for even plastic keys with the right combinations open doors.

We tend to want to open the door with our beautiful old key, but it doesn't fit. There are changes in the lock. Families' needs are changing. The numbers of care givers, teachers, and directors needed to respond to the families' needs keep escalating. Our traditional sources of people to staff the centers and schools keep shrinking. Our demands skyrocket for quality servies, quality teacher education, quality continuing education, quality technical assistance for establishing, maintaining and monitoring quality services.

To use our innovation key wisely we must be sensitive to and realistic about the demographics representing the changing needs of children and families. See Ellen Galinsky's "Investing in Quality Child Care: A Report for AT&T" (1985) for statistics which demand broad based legislative and corporate attention at the community, state, and national levels. Our innovations must include new ways and means of getting this information out to the public at large. A challenge we face as early childhood professionals is to help the officials who have the money and resources to recognize the value of our profession, people who can design and implement quality programs for families through direct service to children. Adequate pay and status must accompany professionalism.

With the ornate old key representing our "tradition of commitment" and the rectangular plastic key representing

132

"innovations", which are designed as responses to the changing needs of families, there also is a third key. I can not describe it to you because it is different in design for each professional. It is the key to personal resources. When the profession is torn by the demands of society to do more for children and families and when there are constant quality decisions to be made about new services which arrive on the scene, then to truly remain professionals, we must keep a perspective which requires personal resourcefulness. The key representing personal resourcefulness is whatever keeps the professional alive and vital to return to the demands of the field. It may be an endeavor totally removed from early education or it may be related to the field. There must be a resource of personal fulfillment. For some, it is the delight of meeting new people, or intense research with a question so intriguing that it seizes the imagination, or the dynamics of interacting with staff members as they revise the curriculum, or the new role expectations when becoming a leader. For each professional, it is more than for the sake of the children that we enter and remain in the profession. When a person holds the key to resourcefulness, there is a sense of ownership. Without hesitation and with pride, the person says, "I am an early childhood professional." We see the problems and the challenges facing our profession, but we have some of the answers; the answers are unlocked by a beautiful, old key representing our "tradition of commitment," by a plastic key representing "innovation and change," and by the keys held in the hands of our colleagues which represent the "personal resources" each brings.

To unlock the door to early childhood professionalism, we must use the three keys we hold in our hands, but we also must help our neighbor search for the lost keys, for our success as a profession lies not only in our own hands, but in the keys our colleagues hold in their hands.

REFERENCES

Galinsky, E., with Friedman, D. E. (1986). Investing in quality child care: A report for AT&T. New York: Bank Street College.

Mosenthal, P. (1986). Defining good and poor reading - The problem of artificial lamp posts. The Reading Teacher, 39, 858.

PUBLICATION BIBLIOGRAPHY

BOOKS:

The Wesleyan Papers: Keeping the Child in Childhood, Editor. North Carolina Wesleyan College, 1983. Also available as an ERIC document.

A Guide to Early Learning. Palo Alto, CA: R. & E. Research Associates, 1982.

Parenting Resource Guide Editor, Bobbie L. Walden. Articles by Dr. Raines, "Do's and Don'ts for Working with Parents and Comunity Volunteers," "How Children Learn and What I Can Do to Help My Child Learn," "Simple Activities Parents Can Do with Their Children." Montgomery, AL: Alabama State Department of Education, 1982.

A Guide to Early Learning in Hale County Kindergartens. Greensboro, AL: Hale County Title I Early Childhood Projects, 1980.

ARTICLES, REVIEWS, RESEARCH REPORTS:

"Teacher Educator Learns from First and Second Grade Readers and Writers." Childhood Education 62 (March/April 1986), pp. 250-64.

"Who Are We in the Lives of Children?" Annual Editions: Early Childhood Education 86/87. Editor, Judy Spitler McKee. Guildford, CN: The Dushkin Publishing Group, 1986.

"Nurturing the Young Scientist's Curiosity." Oklahoma Children 11 (August 1986), pp. 9-10.

with Kay Grant. "Let the Children Sing." Oklahoma Children 11 (November 1985), pp 6-7.

"Standardization, Uniqueness and Multi-cultural Awareness." Oklahoma Children 10 (February 1985), p.8.

"Comments from an Interview with Dr. Benjamin Spock." Oklahoma Children 10 (August 1985), pp. 4-5.

"Three uniquely Different Approaches to Improvement of Teacher Development and Education." National Association of Early Childhood Teacher Educators Bulletin. 7 (Winter 1986), pp 5-6.

with S. Nicholson, K. Castle, and J. Franks-Doebler. "A Position Statement on Quality Programs for Four Year Olds in Public Schools." Dimensions. 14 (April 1986), pp. 29-30.

"Who Are We in the Lives of Children?" Young Children. 39 (March 1984), pp 9-12.

"Inviting Parents into the Young Child's World: Book Review." Young Children. 41 (November 1985), pp 59-60.

"Who Are We in the Lives of Children?" Annual Editions: Early Childhood Education 85/86. Editor, Judy Spitler McKee. Guildford, CN: The Dushkin Publishing Group, 1984.

Abstract of The Wesleyan Papers: Keeping the Child in Childhood. Resources in Education. ERIC Clearinghouse on Elementary and Early Childhood Education. June 1984. ED 239739 for full document.

"Asking Children to Think Again." Rocky Mount, NC: Rocky Mount Telegram. (May 15, 1983), p. 20.

"Can I, Can I? Developing Children's Sense of Autonomy." North Carolina Association for the Education of Young Children, NC-AEYS NEWS, (April 1983), pp 1,8.

"Kindergartners and First Graders Learn to Write." Research report and Audiotape of Presentation to international study conference of the Association for Childhood Education International, Cleveland, OH. (Presentation selected as a featured report by the Teacher Education Committee.) Washington, D. C.: ACEI, 1983.

"Developing Professionalism: Shared Responsibility." Childhood Education. 59 (January/February 1983), pp. 151-153.

"Good Beginnings: Teacher Success Stories." The Reading Teacher. 36 (December 1982), pp. 320-321.

"The Way I See It: Teachers Must Not Be Intimidated." Journal of Educational Leadership. 39 (March 1983), p. 447.

"An Account of Meaningful Mathematics." Childhood Education. 57 (January/February 1981), pp. 165-166.

"For Parents - Holiday Geometry." Classroom Activities. 2 (Fall 1982), p. 3.

"Educating the Young Thinker: Book Review." Childhood Education, 57 (November/December 1980), p. 120.

"Fundamentals of Early Childhood Education: Book Review." Capstone Journal of Education, 1 (December 1980), pp. 62-63.

"Listening-Thinking Tasks in Language Arts Materials." Resources in Education, 15:7 (August 1980), Bethesda, Maryland. ERIC REPRODUCTION SERVICES Ed 182756.

"Listening-Thinking Tasks in Selected Language Arts Materials." Dissertation Abstracts International, 40 (December 1979), 3095-3096A.

"Building on the Strength of Listening Development." Teacher Education, 7 (Spring 1978), pp. 121-123.

"Day Care and the One-Winged Chinese Bird." The Record, 4 (August 1978), pp. 33-36.

PROJECT REPORTS:

"Low Cost and No Cost Faculty Development Projects, Sabbaticals and Release Time." Faculty Development Report. Faculty Council, North Carolina Wesleyan College, 1982.

"Kindergarten Education," with other researcher. Report on Curricula and Support Services. Birmingham, AL: Jefferson County Schools, 1980.

Project Impact: Psycho-Educational Resource Program. "A Parent and Child Project," Knoxville, TN: Knox County Schools and East Tennessee Children's Rehabilitation Center, 1975.

Self-Assessment and Program Validation Reports. Knox County Head Start. Knox ville, TN. Knox County Schools and Knoxville-Knox County community Action Commission. Program Grants, Component Reports on Parent Involvement, Social Services, Health and Nutrition, and Education. Curriculum Guides, Parent Newsletters, Job Description Manuals, Volunteer Training Guides, Play and Playground Designs. 1973-76.

Parent's Directory of Community Services and Resources. Knoxville, TN: Knox County Schools, 1972.

Carol Seefeldt

AUTOBIOGRAPHICAL SKETCH OF
CAROL SEEFELDT

Carol Seefeldt is Professor of Education at the Institute for Child Study, University of Maryland where she received the Distinguished Scholar/Teacher Award. She has worked in the field of early childhood education for over 30 years. Her first teaching job was part-time work in a child care center while as an undergraduate in early childhood education at the University of Wisconsin, Milwaukee. After receiving the B.A., she taught first grade in the non-graded primary units of Milwaukee, Wisconsin, St. Louis, Missouri, and Granite City, Illinois.

In Temple Terrace, Florida, Carol Seefeldt opened and taught a private, church-related kindergarten program. She completed her masters' degree in early childhood education at the University of South Florida in Tampa, and the Ph. D. at Florida State University.

In Florida, Dr. Seefeldt served as a Regional Training Officer for Project Head Start and directed training programs for teachers of migrant children and Head Start teachers. Other experiences in Florida included consulting with school systems, child care programs and work with Florida's Association for Children Under Six.

Current research interests include studies of children's attitudes toward the elderly and elders attitudes toward children. Research on the effects of contact between generations and intergenerational attitudes in the cultures in Korea, China, Paraguay, and the Aleutian Islands, has been completed. Other research focuses on early childhood curriculum evaluation, including a five-year longitudinal study of Montessori programs in Arlington, Virginia, and an evaluation of social and emotional outcomes in open space classrooms in Maryland. Evaluation of safety curricula for young children have also been completed. A study exploring the social and emotional outcomes of participation in compotitive activities for young children is currently in process.

Ten textbooks have been authored by Carol Seefeldt. These include: Early Childhood Education: An Introduction, co-authored with Nita Barbour, Social Studies for the Preschool/Primary Child and The Early Childhood Curriculum: A Review of the Research. Articles have been published in Young Children, Childhood Education, Educational Gerontology, Gerontologists, Today's Education, Day Care and Early Years, Principal, Educational Leadership and other journals.

Carol Seefeldt is active in the National Association for the Education of Young Children and the Association for Childhood Education International. She has served as president of the Maryland AEYC. She continues to work with school systems, child care programs and speaks, lectures, and consults throughout the country.

DEWEY'S INFLUENCE

The philosophy of John Dewey has had the most significant impact on my life. During the early 1950's, many of the early childhood faculty at Wisconsin State College had been students of John Dewey. These professors, inspired by the philosophy of Dewey, instilled in their students a commitment for the education of the whole child and a belief that education is a freeing of individual capacity in a progressive growth directed toward social aims.

It wasn't just the ideas of Dewey that impressed me . It was the impact of experiencing these ideas as curriculum. The supervisor of elementary education in the Milwaukee schools, another disciple of Dewey, was a double specialist. She took theory and translated it into practice and in turn, took practice and translated it into theory.

Visiting in my primary classroom, the supervisor noted the absence of a sand and water table. "Do you know how to order a sand table?" she asked, "or is a sand table missing because you do not know how to use sand as a teaching tool? If this is the case, I'll be delighted to come next week and teach you how to use sand and water as materials for learning." Well, the next week both a sand and water table became well-used fixtures in the classroom without her help.

Firm in her belief that children need to think in order to learn and learn to think, she once removed all of the ditto machines from the elementary schools. She claimed, "I was seeing too many ditto sheets on the walls of too many schools. We can't afford children who only know how to follow directions. The machines will go back, but only when they can be used appropriately." Her conviction that children needed to learn to hold an image in their minds, and then to represent that image in symbols for others to gain meaning from, guided her actions. Her dedication to protecting children's rights to appropriate educational experiences, and her courage to act on her dedication, continue to guide.

When Head Start was initiated in the 1960's, it seemed as if our nation had finally embraced the philosophy of Dewey. Through Head Start, Dewey's idea of education designed to "discount the effects of economic inequalities, and secure to the wards of the nation equality of equipment for their future careers" would be realized. Here was a program that recognized the value of early educational experiences of children. The whole child, in the context of the family and the community, would be respected.

Many of the original aims of Head Start have been achieved. Communities changed. Social and medical services were made available to more children and their families. The educational system became more responsive to the needs of all of the children in the community. Parents, after becoming involved in their children's Head Start program, continued to be involved in the children's education. And children achieved!

Yet much remains. Too many eligible children are not in Head Start. Today it is estimated that more than 40% of children in public school could be categorized as "at risk." Children of teen parents, of new immigrants, or economically deprived, the percentage of children at educational risk is increasing. It is predicted that fewer and fewer of these children will complete high school. When we know Head Start works, expecially for these children who are at risk of failing, it seems ludicrous to permit any curtailment of the program.

Dewey's call for "adequate provision of school facilities, and such supplementation of family resources as will enable youth to take advantage of them, and modification of traditional ideas of culture, traditional subjects of study, and traditional methods of teaching and discipline until all children are equipped to be masters of their own economic and social careers" has yet to be fully realized through Head Start.

Dewey's philosophy could also guide early childhood educators in their efforts to protect all our children from other pressures. The demands for early academic achievement and narrowly conceived gains on standardized tests continue to interrupt children's lives and opportunity to learn. Dewey wrote, "Democracy cannot flourish where the chief influences in selecting subject matter are utilitarian ends...the

140

notion that the essentials of elementary education are the three R's mechanically treated, is based upon ignorance of the essentials needed for the realization of democratic ideas."

Yet the future for children could be bright. If Dewey's idea of education as a continuing progression is accurate, then it would seem we could achieve whatever we desire for our children. First, there is the growing recognition that early educational experiences are not only good for children but for all of society. True, the documented payoffs of early education may add pressures on children - for achievement, for solving all of society's problems - but they also mean an increased interest, acceptance and the possibility of increased resources for young children and their education.

Some of this increased interest is reflected in the large numbers of publications focusing on children. Our knowledge of children, how they grow, learn, and develop, increases daily. Not only do we know more about children, but this knowledge is widely disseminated through the press and media.

Technology has added wondrous benefits to our lives and the lives of our children. Advances in medicine, travel and communication continue to enhance our lives and expand our horizons. In recalling my first year of teaching, I remember schools were closed for nearly 6 weeks as a polio epidemic raged. No longer do we fear polio, measles or other childhood diseases that devastated children's lives in the past.

Because of technology, we can fulfill our humanness and stay close to one another. Children and their grandparents are able to develop close, caring relationships through the mail, telephone and readily available, quick travel. In our work on children's attitudes toward the elderly, we found that children and grandparents do spend time together even though they may live far from one another. Both grandparents and children report spending vacations together, visiting back and forth across the country, and speaking to one another on the telephone frequently. All possible because of technology.

The computer will increase our potential. Freeing us from time-consuming tasks, computers will permit us to spend more time with one another in human pursuits. Perhaps the computer will free us to finally be able to devote ourselves to eliminating international jealousy and animosity, and to spending more time nurturing those things that bind people together in cooperative human pursuits apart from geographical limitations.

Professionally, the field of early childhood education has made great strides. Through the national Association for the Education of Young Children, teacher education guidelines have been developed and accepted as requirements by the national Council for Accreditation of Teacher Education. These guidelines, now requirements of programs seeking NCATE accreditation, will do much to strengthen teacher preparation In early childhood education.

The Center Accreditation Program, a voluntary program of accreditation for child care, nursery and other preschools, is another indication of the professionalism of the field of early childhood education. Rather than waiting for the government or some other agency to regulate early childhood programs, the profession took the initiative by setting standards and criteria for excellence. The CAP has done much to enhance and improve the quality of experiences children and their families receive.

NAEYC's statements of Developmentally Appropriate Practices can be viewed as a milestone in improving the quality of early childhood education. These blunt statements describing appropriate and inappropriate practices serve as definitions. Once defined, a thing becomes real. Already researchers are using these statements as definitions of variables. Advocates are using these statements as definitions as they testify before legislators or in designing legislation affecting early childhood education.

Astonishing progress characterizes the more than 30 years I have been involved in early childhood education, and progress continues to accelerate. Whether this progress means the improvement of the quality of life for future generations of children, is uncertain. Dewey pointed out that as societies become more complex in structure and resources, the dangers of creating Inequalities between groups of people, and a split between learning through experiences and the formal learning of the school, become greater. We do have knowledge, technology and a growing profession of dedicated early childhood educators to enable us, if we desire, to create a society which "makes provision for participation in its good for all its members on equal terms and which secures flexible readjustment of its institutions through interaction of the different forms of associated life." The future certainly is in our knowledgeable and professional hands.

SELECTED PUBLICATION BIBLIOGRAPHY

BOOKS:

Seefeldt, C. (1987). Curriculum Research related to Early Childhood Education. New York: Teachers College Press.

Seefeldt, C. & Barbour, N. (1986). Early Childhood Education: An Introduction. Columbus, Ohio: Charles E. Merrill.

Seefeldt, C. (1985). Social Studies for the Preschool-Primary Child. (2nd Edition). Columbus Ohio: Charles E. Merrill.

Seefeldt, C. (1980). Curriculum for Preschools. Columbus, Ohio: Charles E. Merrill.

Seefeldt, C. (1980). Teaching Young Children. Englewood Cliffs, N. J.: Prentice-Hall.

Seefeldt, C. (1976). Curriculum for the Preschool-Primary Child. A Review of the Research. Columbus, Ohio: Charles E. Merrill.

JOURNAL ARTICLES:

Seefeldt, C., & Montgomery, L. (1986). The relation between perceived supervisory style and behavior of child care teachers. Child Care Quarterly, 15, 4, 251-259.

Seefeldt, C. (1985). Parent involvement: Support or stress? Childhood Education, 62, 2, 98-103.

Seefeldt, C., & Hildebrand, J. (1986). The relation between teacher burnout and quality of child care. Child Care Quarterly, 15, 2. (In Press).

Seefeldt, C. (1985). Today's kindergarten: Pleasure or pressure?, Principal, 64, 5, 12-16.

Seefeldt, C., & Tinney, S. (1985). Dinosaurs: The past is present. Young Children, 40, 4, 20-24.

Seefeldt, C., & Smalz, I. (1985). Let me teach. Principal, 64, 4, 40-43.

Seefeldt, C. (1984). Children's attitudes toward the elderly: A cross cultural comparison. International Journal of Aging and Human Development, 19, 4, 321-330. Indexed in Inventory of Marriage and Family Literature, Vol. X, 1985.

Seefeldt, C. (1984). What's in a name? Young Children, 39, 5, 24-54. Reprinted in: First School Years.

Seefeldt, C. (1983). The new arrivals. Childhood Education, 60, 2, 74-76.

Seefeldt, C., & Jantz, R. K. (1982). Elders attitudes toward children. Educational Gerontology, 8, 493-506.

Seefeldt, C. (1982). How elders view children. Children Today, 11, 2, 16-21.

Seefeldt, C. (1982). I pledge. Childhood Education, 58, 5, 308-311.

Seefeldt, C. (1981). Social and emotional adjustment of first grade children with and without Montessori preschool experience. Child Study Journal, 11, 4, 231-246.

Seefeldt, C. & Tafoya, E. (1981). Children's attitudes toward the elderly: Native Alaskan and the mainland United States. International Journal of Marriage and the Family, 11, 1, 15-24. Reprinted in: International Journal of Sociology of the Family, 1981, 11, 1, 15.

Seefeldt, C. (1981). Math in a button box. Day Care and Early Education, Spring, 53-57.

Seefeldt, C., Jantz, R. K., Galper A., & Serock, K. (1981). Healthy, happy and old: Children learn about the elderly. Educational Gerontology, 7, 79-87. Indexed in: Inventory of Marriage and the Family, Vol. VIII, 1982.

Seefeldt, C. (1979). The effects of a program designed to increase children's perceptions of texture. Studies in Art Education, 20, 2, 40-45.

Jantz, R. K., & Seefeldt, C. (1979). Oh no! Not me, I'm not getting old! Life and Health, March, 33-39.

Seefeldt, C., Serock, K., Galper, A., & Jantz, R. K. (1978). The coming of age in children's literature. Childhood Education, 4, 3, 123-128. Reprinted in: Education Digest, April, 1978, 56-59.

Ross, S. & Seefeldt, C. (1978). Young children in traffic: How will they cope? Young Children, 33, 4, 68-73.

Seefeldt, C., Jantz, R. K., Galper, A., & Serock, K. (1977). Using pictures to assess children's attitudes toward the elderly. The Gerontologist, 17, 6, 506-513. Reprinted in: D. H. Olson (Ed.) Inventory of Marriage and the Family Literature. Vol. V, St. Paul: University of Minnesota, Family Social Science, 1977-1978.

Seefeldt, C., Jantz, R. K., Galper, A., & Serock, K. (1977). Children's attitudes toward the elderly: Curriculum implications. Educational Gerontologist, 2, 1, 301-311.

Seefeldt, C. (1977). Young and old together. Children Today, 6, 1, 21-26. Reprinted in: Guided Study Course, University of Iowa, Center for Credit, 1979. Reprinted in: Magazine Reprints: International Press and Publication Service Communication Agency.

Seefeldt, C., Serock, K., Jantz, R. K., & Galper, A. (1977). As children see old folks. Today's Education, 66, 2, 70-74. Reprinted in: Focus: Aging, Sluice Dock, Guilford, Ct. Duskin Publishing Group, Inc., 1978.

Goetz, J. & Seefeldt, C. (1975). Woodworking: An industrial arts unit for young children. Man, Society and Technology, 34, 8, 235-239.

Seefeldt, C. (1975). Is today tomorrow? History for young children. Young Children, 30, 2, 99-105. Reprinted in: Milwaukee Public Schools Teachers' Bulletin, 1976. Also: Early Childhood Education, New York: Doctorate Association of New York Educators, Avery Publishing Group, 1978.

Seefeldt, C. (1973). Open spaces-closed learning? Educational Leadership, 20, 4, 353-361. Reprinted in: L. Chamberlin and R. Cote (eds.) The Emerging School. New York: Macmillan & Co. 1974. Also: A. Gayles, Proven and Promising Educational Innovations in Secondary Education, Columbus, Ohio: Charles E. Merrill, 1974. Also: P. H. Martorell, Social Studies: Theory Into Practice, New York: Harper & Row, 1975.

Seefeldt, C. (1972). Boxes are to build a curriculum. Young Children, 28, 1, 4-15. Reprinted in: News for Hillsborough Teachers, Tampa, Florida, 1973. Also: Resources for Education, ERIC, Urbana, Illinois, 1975.

Seefeldt, C. (1972). Toward appreciation. Elementary English, 49, 5, 787-797.

Seefeldt, C. (1978). My Own Safety Story, Falls Church, VA: American Automobile Association. Revised 1979, 1980.

Seefeldt, C. (1975). For Teachers: Traffic Safety Guides, 1975-1976. Falls Church, VA: American Automobile Association. Revised 1976, 1978, 1981.

Seefeldt, C. & Dittmann, L. (1975). Day Care: Family Day Care No. 9, Washington, D. C.: Office of Child Development, U. S. Department of Health, Education and Welfare.

Seefeldt, C. (1974). Planning and Implementing Home Based Child Development Programs. Washington, D. C.: Office of Child Development, U. S. Department of Health, Education and Welfare.

ALBERT SHANKER

AUTOBIOGRAPHICAL SKETCH OF
ALBERT SHANKER

Albert Shanker has been president of the American Federation of Teachers, AFL-CIO, since 1974. Since assuming the presidency of the AFT, the union's membership has grown to 630,000, a 40 percent increase in 10 years.

In addition to serving as AFT president, Mr. Shanker is vice president of the AFL-CIO where he ranks fourth in seniority on the Executive Council.

Mr. Shanker's stature in the education and labor movement took hold when he was elected president of the United Federation of Teachers, an AFT affiliate in New York City. He resigned that position on January 1, 1986, to devote his full attention to national concerns.

Since 1981, he has been president of the International Federation of Free Teachers' Unions (IFFTU), headquartered in Brussels, an organization of teacher unions in the democratic countries.

Mr. Shanker serves on the Carnegie Forum on Education and the Economy's Task Force on Teaching As A Profession and was named to the National Academy of Education.

He is president of the AFL-CIO Department of Professional Employees. The teacher union leader is also a vice president of the New York State AFL-CIO.

Mr. Shanker has been secretary of the Jewish Labor Committee, an honorary vice chairman of the American Trade Union Council for Histadrut and a member of the National Board of Directors of the National Committee for Labor Israel. An ardent fighter for civil and human rights, he has served on the Boards of the A. Philip Randolph Institute, the League for Industrial Democracy, the International Rescue Committee and the Committee for the Defense of Soviet Political Prisoners. He serves on advisory councils of the Population Institute and the Committee for Multilateral Trade Negotiations. He is a member of the Trilateral Commission and the Committee for the Free World. He has served as an American delegate to several international conferences on Soviet Jewry. Mr. Shanker also serves on advisory boards for the Committee for International Human Rights, the Committee for Economic Development and the Education Commission of the States.

Also, Mr. Shanker is on the Yale School of Management Advisory Board, the Joint Council on Economic Education, the Dropout Prevention Fund, the Family Policy Panel, the National Council on Science and Technology of the American Association for Advancement of Science's Project 2061, the Education Advisory Council of the Metropolitan Life Foundation, the Institute for Teaching and Education Study and the Advisory Panel of Public School Early Childhood Study. He also serves on the National Commission on Excellence in Educational Administration.

For the past 16 years, Mr. Shanker has written a weekly column, "Where We Stand," on education, labor, political and human rights issues, which appears in the Week in Review, political section of the Sunday New York Times and is picked up by some 60 papers across the country. He is a frequent contributor to national magazines and education journals, often testifies before Congressional committees on education, labor, urban and human rights matters and speaks at numerous conferences and seminars in this country and abroad.

Mr. Shanker has been recognized by several magazines -- The New Republic, Phi Delta Kappan, Harper's and Washington Monthly -- as a statesman in his field.

In May, the New York State Board of Regents presented Mr. Shanker with the James E. Allen, Jr., Memorial Award for Distinguished Service to Education, the highest honor of its kind in New York.

He is a frequent guest on such nationally broadcast news and public affairs programs as "Meet the Press," "Face the Nation," "It's Your Business," "Good Morning America," "The Larry King Show," "CBS Morning News," "Today," and "This Week with David Brinkley."

Mr. Shanker was born in New York City in 1928 and educated at the city's public schools, including Stuyvesant High School. He was graduated with honors in philosophy from the University of Illinois and completed course requirements for the Ph.D. at Columbia University. Among his awards are an honorary doctorate in pedagogy from Rhode Island College, an honorary doctorate in humane letters from the City University of New York and Adelphi University, the Creative Leadership Award of the New York University School of Education, Health, Nursing and Arts Professions, and the Heritage of Liberty Award of the Anti-

148

Defamation League of B'nai B'rith. In May, 1985 he received a Medal for Distinguished Service (for contributions in education) from Columbia University Teachers College.

He also serves on the President's Committee on Employment of the Handicapped and is an associate for the Gannett Center for Media Studies at Columbia University in New York.

Mr. Shanker played a strong role in the founding of the UFT (The New York local) in its fight for collective bargaining, in the negotiation of its earliest contracts more than 20 years ago (the models for subsequent teacher contracts all around the country), in its strikes (serving time in jail for violating New York's collective bargaining statutes) -- and in its successes.

From teacher salaries of $2,500 a year when he started teaching junior high school math in 1952, he has brought New York City teachers up to a maximum of $38,050 even while facing a decade-long city fiscal crisis. Along the way were major improvements in health and welfare benefits, pensions and job protection, not only for some 60,000 city teachers but also for 10,000 classroom paraprofessionals, mostly minority women, for whom Shanker negotiated a successful college-career ladder that leads to teaching jobs.

In recent years, Mr. Shanker has been prominent in urging teachers to take seriously the various reports sharply critical of American education and to play a strong role in education reform -- even to the point of being willing to discuss issues teachers long have shunned, including differentiated salary schedules and other proposals that businessmen, governors and educators have put forth. He has long used the column, "Where We Stand," to anticipate education trends, reveal shortcomings, propose solutions. In fact, there was little in "A Nation at Risk," the report of the National Commission on Excellence in Education, which hadn't already appeared in the weekly Shanker column. He'd called for tougher courses, standards and discipline, for a return to clear teaching of a common core of democratic values, for testing not only students but teacher candidates as well, for vastly improved starting and career salaries to attract the best and brightest into teaching -- and he'd warned that American schools were not standing up to the competition, that future jobs would go begging while poorly educated workers were unemployed.

Mr. Shanker, a gourmet cook and baker when time permits, is

married to the former Edith Gerber, who taught school with him in the 1950s. They have three children, Adam, Jennie and Michael, and live in Mamaroneck, New York.

WALL MENDING
AND
EDUCATION REFORM

What our country's education reform movement desperately needs now is a flight of imagination that will take us beyond old assumptions. Much of what has already been done to improve our schools reminds me of the neighbor that Robert Frost described in "Mending Wall." He went on repairing the boundary wall every year because he could never get himself to critically examine the truism that his father had passed down to him that "Good fences make good neighbors."

In the same way, many well-intentioned reformers have tried to repair our education system on the basis of their fathers' and grandfathers' assumptions of what constitutes a good school. The effect of most of what we've done is to try to restore the quality of "the good old days," what most of our classrooms were like back in the 40's and 50's.

For example, we've tightened up the looseness brought in during the free-wheeling 60's and early 70's. We've gone back to state-mandated solid curriculums and more required subjects, along with tests of basic skills. Students are no longer going to be allowed to substitute a course on comic books for a course with Dickens and Shakespeare on the reading list. In essence, students will have to do a lot more than put in seat time to get a diploma.

Teachers have gotten the same treatment. Many states and communities have instituted tests to determine if the faculty's college degrees mean anything and if teachers really know at least the basics of what they're supposedly teaching their students. And state authorities no longer intend to take chances about what is going on in the classroom. Therefore, they have mandated highly structured curriculums, with the texts to be used and the tests to be given all spelled out. Teachers might be able to pass basic skills tests, but they aren't going to be trusted by the authorities to do their own thing in the classroom.

Some of this tightening-up is a welcome and long overdue corrective to the slackness of the last two decades. But we need to see clearly what we'll be getting in the end for our effort.

Grandma and Grandpa would find our "reformed" schools familiar, the time-tested model of what education is supposed to be. The corridors are lined with orderly, self-contained classrooms in which, because of large class sizes, teachers are forced to do a great deal of lecturing to relatively passive students who are expected to absorb and then repeat, on periodic tests, large chunks of knowledge specified by detailed, mandated curriculums. There is little time and opportunity for reflection, discussion or variations of pedagogical approaches. "X" amount of material has to be covered each day before the bell rings and sends the class off to another subject.

There is a great deal to be said for order and for a solid curriculum. And the schools I've described continue to work well for many bright and motivated students, as they did in the past. But, even in their heyday, such schools also produced dropout rates of up to 70 percent, and that at a time in the late 40s and 50s when family support systems were far stronger than they are today.

If we do nothing else but make our standards tougher, we will likely encourage a few now lackadaisical students to try harder. But marginal students who fail or can barely function in a loose system will be driven out in increasing numbers as school gets tougher. Urban dropout rates that are now about 40 or 50 percent will soar to 70 or 80 percent. We will have the "good old days" with a vengeance. If most of the reforms now in force or on the table for consideration will fail to solve the educational problems of the vast majority of students so will they fail to defuse the demographic time bomb ticking away in our schools. Projections tell us that we will have to replace about half of our nation's 2.2 million teachers within the next decade. This means that our schools will have to recruit and retain about 24 percent of each college graduating class in the next seven to ten years -- an utterly unrealistic expectation, particularly since only about 6 percent of last year's entering freshmen expressed an interest in teaching.

Many school districts have made good-faith efforts to make teaching a more attractive profession. Though reform has brought

151

about significant and long-delayed increases in salaries, they are still nowhere near a professional level, averaging nationwide about $26,000 after 15 years of service! To compete with the private sector, salaries would have to be increased by at least 50%, which would mean at least a staggering $30 billion increase in the nation's annual education budget -- for one item. And, in shortage areas like math and science, there is simply no way that an IBM or General Electric will allow itself to be outbid by the local school district for the talent available in those disciplines.

But this is the problem we face merely to retain current staff levels. Consider, then, the enormity of the task of improving teachers' working conditions, for example, or of finding more personnel along with the money to pay them to lower class sizes to optimum levels.

If the picture is bleak, it is largely so because many of our reformers are trying to "mend" our schools instead of rethinking or restructuring them. The poverty of resources that many of our schools suffer is matched by a poverty of imagination. We find it hard to go beyond our parents' idea of what a school is like. If we have to start our system from scratch would we really think that the best proposal is to put large numbers of students in a room and expect them to sit quietly for five or six hours and listen attentively as an adult lectures to them for most of that time? And would we really expect to recruit and retain large numbers of able professionals who would want to spend their careers "performing" without respite, burdened with bureaucratic, non-teaching chores, with little or no stimulation from an ongoing collegial exchange of ideas with other professionals?

The 1986 Carnegie report, A Nation Prepared, convincingly argued that in order to maintain our political system and our standard of living, our schools would have to reach a majority of students at a higher intellectual level than ever before. Clearly, this can't be done with carbon copies of even the best schools of the 40's and 50's. We have to recognize that most students can't learn effectively by listening passively to a teacher lecture and taking notes one period after another.

We need to imagine other school structures and other learning strategies. We need to work out ways of providing for more small group work or one-on-one coaching. We need to make greater use of technology, particularly computers and video tapes. We need to try variations of the structure of the school year and the length of courses. We need to try more peer tutoring. We need to develop more learning opportunities in partnership with industry and the business community. Of course, these ideas in no way exhaust the possibilities. But we need to begin with the assumption that new visions are essential, that the old structures are a dead end.

The same holds true for the teaching profession. The old incentives will no longer serve to staff our schools with enough high-quality personnel. Professional level salaries will be essential but not sufficient in themselves. We need to scrap our prevailing highly bureaucratic, top-down management, factory-style education system where the teachers are seen as hardly more than assembly-line workers who have to be supervised to death and told what to do at almost every turn. Our best college graduates expect something more. We need to turn our schools into professional workplaces where highly trained personnel have control over their working lives -- the opportunity to choose materials, develop curriculums, attempt varying teaching strategies and regularly share ideas with colleagues. In other words, teachers need the kind of responsibility, stimulation and resources that other professionals assume are givens of their working lives.

Our schools have a history of great achievement. They served our nation well in an industrial society. But our economy has changed and so have our expectations. We cannot accept the prospect of a large underclass of uneducated or minimally educated citizens. We need to make that first difficult leap of the imagination and look behind our ancestors' assumptions. Only then will the light go on.

SELECTED PUBLICATION BIBLIOGRAPHY

"Capitalism in the Classroom," Crain's New York Business, April 1, 1985.

"Collective Bargaining With Educational Standards," Education on Trial, ed. by William J. Johnston, San Francisco, 1985.

"Early Childhood Education and the Public Schools," Family and Work, edited by Hewlett, Ilchman and Sweeney, Cambridge, 1987.

"Learning Disabilities," (Review), The New Leader, April 22, 1985.

"Schlomo Delivered," The Forward, October 11, 1985.

"Teacher Bargaining: More Boon Than Bane," (Review), CER Newsletter, Vol. 3, #2.

"The Lot of Teachers," National Lampoon, November, 1985.

The Making of a Profession, Publication of the American Federation of Teachers, 1985.

"The Revolution That's Overdue," Phi Delta Kappan, January, 1985.

"Time to Turn Teaching Upside Down," The Orlando Sentinel, September 21, 1986.

Verl M. Short

AUTOBIOGRAPHICAL SKETCH OF
VERL M. SHORT

Verl M. Short was born in Eureka, California, on August 7, 1928. He is currently a professor of education at West Georgia College, Carrollton, Georgia. His major area of expertise is in the field of early childhood education. Verl Short was a classroom teacher for eight years, school administrator for six years, and a college professor and administrator for the past twenty years. He is currently also serving as the President of the Association for Childhood Education International. Dr. Short earned his A.B. from the University of Pacific, M.A. from Sacramento State College, and Ed.D. from Northern Illinois University. His mentors of long-standing were his teaching mother, Ruth K. Short, and Marc Jantzen from the University of Pacific. The former taught him all she knew about classroom teaching and the latter introduced him to the social importance of becoming a teacher.

A REVIEW OF SELECTED
CONTEMPORARY ISSUES IN EARLY
CHILDHOOD EDUCATION

Educators tend to practice their philosophy in lieu of examining it regularly. And since teachers change their educational practices from time-to-time, they also change philosophies. One has to also work extremely hard to make sure that his philosophy is practiced on a daily basis. Considering the educational climate and continuous social and technological changes in the United States today, that often is a real challenge for a teacher at any level.

Some of the significant changes that have occurred in the last thirty-five years, that have affected young children, have been numerous to say the least. The following selections were certainly important and noteworthy.

1. The aftereffects of World War II, Korea, and Viet Nam certainly have created uncertainty in this world and severe mental health concerns for the adult survivors and their children. A peaceful world seems as illusive as ever for mankind.

2. The advent of television has made a tremendous

impact on children and their understanding of the world around them. The loss of innocence and the concern about the disappearance of childhood can easily be traced to this particular medium. On the other hand, the world has entered the young child's home with the turn of a knob.

3. Integrating the public schools made a significant change in the education for all our young children in the United States. Unfortunately, much more must still be accomplished in this area as minorities struggle to achieve their rightful place in this society.

4. The mobility of the American society has caused parents to be far removed from their extended families. Thus, the nuclear family has few resources available in time of need. This has created a lot of family stress and certainly has had an effect on the high divorce rate in this country.

5. Basic economics and the women's movement have combined to provide more working mothers not only greater career opportunities, but changing parenting roles for both sexes. Children have subsequently found themselves in more child care programming and sometimes even a part of the latch key syndrome. Rising inflation has also caused parents to consciously reduce the size of their families. The cost of raising a child today has caused married adults to weigh the merits involved more cautiously.

A lot of these changes mean that parents and teachers now need to unite and become a part of a team to help provide young children the best supportive environment possible. A warm parent or teacher cares about the child, expresses affection, frequently puts the child's needs first, shows enthusiasm for the child's activities, and responds sensitively and empathically to a child's feelings. Naturally, few parents or teachers are constantly loving and warm toward their children, but it is the goal they must strive to attain in order for their children to become everything that they can be in one short lifetime.

It has long been understood that education's greatest ally is the students we serve. They are our daily ambassadors that enter each of their homes after school and sing the praises of our work. This is particularly true with young children. They have a blinding trust in what we say and do. That is why we serve as models for them whether we like it or not. A happy child often wins parental support for what we do in the classroom and school.

On the other hand, education's greatest enemy is ignorance. Many people simply do not know the school program, goals, evaluation process, and even the teacher of their children. Educators have never been effective in the area of public relations. It is no wonder that schooling is often compared with the business model. People simply understand business a great deal more than they understand how our schools operate. Education will never achieve the place it deserves in our society until we can explain our mission and teaching methods to the public we serve.

Parent education is one area of socialization that needs a great deal more nourishing in our modern society. It must include such topic areas as prenatal care, birthing, child development, nutrition and drug education, school programming, children and television, and much more. Unfortunately, very few monies and education efforts have been directed toward this critical social need.

Many past leaders in education have left their mark on young children. Many of them have never been formally recognized. Educators literally stand on the shoulders of the achievement of those who went before them in history. Some leaders that have provided all of us some very broad shoulders to stand on were: Johann Amos Comenius, Martin Luther, Johann Heinrich Pestalozzi, Friedrich Froebel, Jean Piaget, Mararethe Schurz, Elizabeth Peabody, Susan Blow, Patty Smith Hill, Margaret McMillan, Erik Erikson, and every great classroom teacher that ever guided students to new heights of personal achievement.

It is sad to note that with this long heritage, public and private schools today are not generally meeting the needs of young children. The program emphasis of each has moved away from being child development centered and toward the teaching of inappropriate skills for the ages of the children being served. It is such a serious problem that most responsible leaders in early childhood are trying to stem the tide of this ill conceived movement. The entire educational process is currently under the control of those promoting accountability. More and more so-called national and state blue ribbon reports have been published which advocate such classroom malpractice. This problem is so pervasive that most educators are finding the struggle awesome to say the least since the legislators in most states are supporting this accountability concept.

In light of all this, it is critical that educators take a hard look at what can be done to best help young children. The changes that seem to be needed the most are the following:

1. making good child care programming available at a reasonable cost through tax supported dollars from local, state, and national governments.

2. providing of parent education on a wide variety of topics through the public schools.

3. returning the educational programs for young children to a developmental approach and thus eliminating current inappropriate activities at the early childhood levels and beyond.

4. hiring of sufficient classroom aides so that every child that needs additional assistance can be sure it is available to him or her In the long run this would be much cheaper than the cost of providing prisons and long term social welfare support. Education of the young child is cost effective.

5. reorganization of our public schools so that there are professional and financial incentives for keeping great teachers in the classroom.

The role of technology in the lives of young children is a lot more complicated than it appears on the surface. No one can really predict its future accurately. Young people serviced by the public school will live their adult lives in the twenty-first century. Most classroom teachers are ill equipped to predict all the types of technology that students will encounter throughout their adult lifetimes. However, teachers can introduce the technology currently available. They can also help students to be open to new ideas, flexible in terms of career education goals, and with the skills to evaluate the long-term effects of developing technology. Lastly, they must assist children to develop the literacy required to deal with the ever changing technology of the future.

There are many challenges confronting the future of children, schools, families, society and world survival. However, the human spirit is very resilient. Challenges have been equally difficult for mankind through recorded history. Based upon this fact alone it is rather easy to predict that many of these modern challenges will be resolved and that new ones, equally difficult, will appear in their place. Mankind has learned to cope with this changing environment, and it is predicted that each new generation will struggle on with a lot of good teachers' help.

PUBLICATION BIBLIOGRAPHY

Authored   - "Department of the Army Orientation Program." Unpublished Masters Thesis, 1959, Sacramento, California.

Co-Authored - Current Salary Practices in Northern Illinois - 1964 - NIU Press, Dekalb, Illinois.

Edited   - Explorations in Selected Problems of Adult Education - 1965 - NIU Press, Dekalb, Illinois.

Co-Authored - Survey of Illinois Colleges Study Relating to the Preparation of School Administrators - 1965 - NIU Press, Dekalb, Illinois.

Co-Edited   - Speaking About Adults and the Continuing Education Process - 1st edition, Sept. 1966, 2nd edition, Feb. 1967 - NIU Press, Dekalb, Illinois.

Authored   - Forecasting Pupil Population - 1967 - NIU Press, DeKalb, Illinois.

Co-Authored - United States Teacher Certification Map (A Guide to Elementary & Secondary State Teacher Requirements) - 1st edition, 1967, 2nd edition, 1969, 3rd edition, 1971 - NIU Press, DeKalb, Illlinois.

Authored   - "Social Studies Reading Material Problems." Florida Reading Quarterly, June, 1968.

Edited   - Florida Reading Quarterly, Book Review Editor, 1968-69.

Authored   - "The KIndergarten Program" - Series of seven articles published in the Pensacola News Journal, March 23 - March 29, 1969.

Authored   - "The first 'R' in the Kindergarten", Florida Reading Quarterly, December, 1969.

Authored   - "The Early Childhood Program" - Series of four articles published in The Halifax Herald, February 10-11, 1970.

Authored - "Greatest Problem Facing Education in Nova Scotia Today," Nova Scotia Teachers Union Newsletter, Vol. 8, No. 11, Jan. 30, 1970.

Co-Authored - "Selection and Training of Adult Educators", Journal of Education, (Nova Scotia), Vol. 19, No. 1, December, 1969.

Co-Authored - "In-Service Teacher Training for Adult Literacy Problems," Journal of Education (Nova Scotia), Volume 19, Number 2, March 1970.

Authored - "Education's Numbers Racket, Let's Take the Number Mystique Out of Education." School Progress, Vol. 39, No. 5, May, 1970.

Edited - Early Childhood Education for Today and Tomorrow, Simon and Schuster, New York, N.Y., 1970, 2nd edition, 1971.

Authored - "Possible Oversupply of Teachers In The 70's?" Nova Scotia Teachers Union Newsletter, Vol. 9, No. 6, November 16, 1970.

Co-Edited - A Selected Collection of Fingerplays and Poems For Use in Early Childhood Education, Nova Scotia Preschool Education Association, Halifax, Nova Scotia, 1971.

Co-Authored - A Big Program For Little People, Nova Scotia Preschool Education Association, Halifax, Nova Scotia, 1971.

Co-Authored - "Don't Sit Still, Jimmy" - Nova Scotia Teachers Union Newsletter, Vol. 10, No. 21, Sept. 15, 1971.

Authored - "The Goals of Early Childhood Education" - Nova Scotia Teachers Union Newsletter, Vol. 10, No. 22, Oct. 15, 1971.

Co-Authored - Handbook of Practice Teaching - Nova Scotia Teachers College Press, Truro, Nova Scotia, 1971.

Authored - "What Is The Open Classroom?" - Nova Scotia Teachers Union Newsletter, The Teacher, Vol. 10, No. 10, Feb. 1, 1972.

Co-Authored - Guiding Your Young Child Through School, Nova Scotia Preschool Education Association, Halifax, Nova Scotia, 1972.

Authored - -"The Open Classroom," Education Canada, Vol. 12, No. 2, June, 1972.

Authored - "Differentiated Staffing And Its Significance To Teacher Education," The Blank, Vol. 1, No. 2, Nova Scotia Teachers College Library, Truro, N.S., June, 1972.

Co-Edited - A Selected Collection of French Materials For Use in Early Childhood Education, Nova Scotia Preschool Education Association, Halifax, Nova Scotia, 1972.

Co-Edited   -   A Point In Time..Readings In Early Childhood Education, MSS, Inc.,
                 New York, N.Y., 1973.

Authored   -   "The Importance of Kindergarten" - Series of seven articles published
                 in the Carroll County Georgian, Nov. 14, 21, 28, Dec. 5, 12, 19, and 26,
                 1974.

Authored   -   "Learning by Helping Others," Childhood Education, Nov.- Dec.,
                 Volume 55, Number 2, 1978.

Co-Edited   -   Young Children and Their Environment. MSS, Inc., New York, N.Y.,
                 1976.

Co-Authored -   The Learning Center Book ... An Integrated Approach. Goodyear Pub.
                 Co., Inc., Pacific Palisades, Calif. (Published in January, 1976).

Co-Authored -   Learning Centers for Everyone. Southeast Educators Services, Inc.,
                 Carrollton, Georgia, 1975.

Co-Authored -   Your Favorite Fingerplays & Poems for the Young Child. Southeast
                 Educators Services, inc., Carrollton, Ga., 1975. (Second edition
                 published in 1977).

Authored   -   My Bicentennial Story Book. Historical Children's Publications, Inc.,
                 Atlanta, Ga., 1975.

Authored   -   My Bicentennial History Book. Historical Children's Publications, inc.,
                 Atlanta, Ga., 1975.

Co-Authored -   Creative Fun for Everyone. Southeast Educators, Inc., Carrollton,
                 Georgia, 1976.

Co-Edited   -   Tips for Teachers...With A Little Help From Our Friends. Georgia
                 Association for Childhood Education, Atlanta, Ga., 1976.

Editor   -   Journal of Humanistic Eduction. Carrollton, Georgia, 1976-1978.

Editor   -   Georgia Association for Childhood Education Newsletter, Carrollton,
                 Georgia, 1977 to 1984.

Co-Authored -   Who Ever Said..an old lemon can't have a new twist. "Southeast
                 Educators, Inc., Carrollton, Georgia, 1980".

Co-Authored -   Selected Readings About Education and the Young Child, Ginn,
                 Lexington, Mass., 1980.

Co-Edited   -   A Bushel of Ideas for the Early Years. GACEI: Carrollton, Ga., 1982.

Co-Edited   -   Curriculum Issues: Early Childhood Education, Ginn Press, Lexington,
                 Mass., 1983.

Authored   -   "The Politics of Education Can Give You a Headache," <u>A.C.E.I.</u> <u>Newsletter</u>, Vol. 54, No. 3, June, 1985.

Authored   -   "Think England in 1986!," <u>A.C.E.I. Newsletter</u>, Vol. 54, No. 5, February, 1986.

Authored   -   "The Making of a Teacher," <u>A.C.E.I. Newsletter</u>, Vol. 54, No. 4, January, 1987.

Co-Authored -   "The English Infant/Primary Schools Revisited," <u>Childhood Education</u>, (Accepted for publication in December, 1987).

Brian Sutton-Smith

AUTOBIOGRAPHICAL SKETCH OF
BRIAN SUTTON-SMITH

Brian Sutton-Smith is Professor of Education in the Graduate School of Education at the University of Pennsylvania where he is Head of the Program of Interdisciplinary Studies in Human Development and Professor of Folklore in the Faculty of Arts and Sciences.

Areas of expertise include developmental psychology and children's folklore, involving children's play and games and forms of artistic expression, particularly drama, narrative and film-making, as well as sibling relationships and sex roles.

He earned a Ph.D. from the University of New Zealand in 1954. He was a Fulbright research scholar with Harold Jones of the Institute of Child Development in Berkeley, California, 1952-53; with David Riesman, University of Chicago, 1953 and with Paul Gump and Fritz Redl at Wayne State University, 1953-54. Mentors include not only these four educators, but others with whom he has worked to include Prof. B. G. Rosenberg, Bowling Green State, Ohio, 1956-67; Prof. John M. Roberts, anthropologist at Cornell from 1960-1967; Prof. Bernard Kaplan, Clark University, 1963 and Dr. Diana Kelly-Byrne, University of Pennsylvania, 1978-87.

CHILDREN'S PLAY

I believe philosophy is more of a temperamental than a cognitive matter as applied to educational praxis. One of my reasons for a life spent pursuing the nature of play and games is my feeling that these are the human domains in which optimism is the outcome. They are constantly investigated for their cognitive or pragmatic outcomes, when the important consequence is their feeling that life has been experienced more vividly and is therefore worth pursuing in its more sober aspects as well.

My interest in children arose during my own teaching career with grade school children in New Zealand from 1942 onwards. My father and grandfather (a saddlesmith in Waikouaiti, New Zealand) were family storytellers, and my first books were children's novels written for the children that I was teaching. With my own imagination thus excited by my students, I became interested in turn in their play and games; and my Ph.D. thesis was an investigation of that topic beginning in 1949.

The significant change in children in my lifetime is the shift from the dominance of group games based on physical skill to solitary (video) or dyadic games (strategy) based on intellectual skill. The solitarization of childhood is my major theme in my book: TOYS AS CULTURE.

My greatest fear is that in striving for achievement and intellectual excellence we will engender an obedience culture, with little opportunity for individual initiative and originality such as has been traditionally afforded through group and solitary play.

Education's greatest ally is the recess period, because it reinvigorates the subject population who can buy the educational stress in return for the opportunity to live vigorously and dynamically with their peers even for short periods of time.

Playmates are the most important agents of socialization because they affirm the child's own impulses and characteristics and vivify the worthwhileness of the human endeavour.

I credit Rousseau, Pestalozzi, Froebel, Dewey and Piaget as benign inflences for children because of their emphasis on the child's own instrumentality. Almost all others have been concerned in one way or another to manipulate the socialization of children for the greater good of various adultcentric purposes. Even Piaget is translated in that way, but that is clearly not his fault. Obviously, mine is a classically "romantic" point of view, but I still find it superior to the alternatives.

My own role in all of this is to show just how much children acquire and revel in through their own play and folklore; and how much their lives are vivified by such indulgences; and more recently, how much they have to lose through the closing out of recess opportunities. I would be quite happy if I could die saying that I had saved recess (children's favorite school subject) for childhood. But I am also opposed to the idealization of play in this century, the widespread attempt to pretend it is a respectful, creative, imaginative activity alone, when in many ways children's play is also a quite rough political way of life for those involved in it. As adults we deceive only ourselves when

166

we romanticize the most romantic phenomenon we have in our hands.

Public schools do well for play largely by inadvertence and fatigue, and for the arts their services are, in general, banal.

More recess, more arts and more technology are all indicated.

The intersect of arts, play and technology has hardly been considered. Each domain has its protagonists, but the future requires them all.

As for some final prognostication, I merely raise my glass to the players of the world, but more importantly to the playful minds, who foresee that is possible to live in some domain of humane liberality this side of the grave and who nourish those under their care in this kindly spirit.

PUBLICATION BIBLIOGRAPHY

BOOKS:

Sutton-Smith, B. Our Street. New Zealand, A. H. Reed, 1950 (Republished Price-Milburn, 1975.

Sutton-Smith, B. The Games of New Zealand Children. Berkeley, CA: University of California Press, 1959. Republished in The Folkgames of Children, 1972, (University of Texas Press).

Sutton-Smith, B. Smitty Does a Bunk. New Zealand, Price-Milburn, 1961. (Republished 1975).

Sutton-Smith, B. and Rosenberg, B. G. The Sibling. New York: Holt, Rinehart and Winston, 1970.

Herron, R. E. and Sutton-Smith, B. Child's Play. New York: Wiley, 1971.

Avedon, E. M. and Sutton-Smith, B. The Study of Games. New York: Wiley, 1971.

Rosenberg, B. G. and Sutton-Smith, B. Sex and Identity. New York: Holt, Rinehart and Winston, 1972.

Sutton-Smith, B. The Folkgames of Children. Austin, Texas: University of Texas Press, 1972.

Sutton-Smith, B. Child Psychology. New York: Appleton-Century, 1973.

Sutton-Smith, B. Readings in Child Psychology. New York: Appleton-Century, 1973.

Sutton-Smith, B. and Sutton-Smith, S. How to Play With Your Children. New York: Hawthorne Books, 1974. (Now E. F. Dutton, Park Avenue, New York, 10016.

Sutton-Smith, B. The Cobbers. New Zealand: Price-Milburn, 1976.

Sutton-Smith, B. (Ed.) Studies in Play and Games. New York: Arno Press, 1976. (Twenty-three republished volumes including the following three books of readings.)

Sutton-Smith, B. (Ed.) The Games of the Americas. Part I and Part II. New York: Arno Press, 1976.

Sutton-Smith, B. (Ed.) A Children's Game Anthology. New York: Arno Press, 1976.

Sutton-Smith, B. (Ed.) The Psychology of Play. New York: Arno Press, 1976.

Sutton-Smith, B. Die Dialektik Des Spiels. West Germany: Verlang Karl Hoffman, Schorndorf, 1978.

Sutton-Smith, B. (Ed.) Play and Learning. New York: Gardner Press, 1979.

Sutton-Smith, B. The Folkstories of Children. Philadelphia: University of Pennsylvania Press, 1981.

Sutton-Smith, B. A History of Children's Play. Philadelphia: University of Pennsylvania Press, 1981.

Sutton-Smith, B. (Ed.) (with Michael Lamb) Sibling Relationships Throughout the Lifespan. Erlbaum, 1982.

Sutton-Smith, B. and Kelly-Byrne, D. The Masks of Play. New York: Leisure Press, 1984.

Sutton-Smith, B. Toys As Culture. New York, Gardner Press, 1986.

Ralph W. Tyler

AUTOBIOGRAPHICAL SKETCH OF
RALPH W. TYLER

I was born in 1902 in Chicago while my father was attending the theological seminary. In 1904, he completed his theological training, and we moved to Nebraska where he was a Congregational minister.

I attended the first kindergarten in Nebraska, established as part of the Demonstration School of the Nebraska State Normal School in Peru, Nebraska. In 1911, we moved from Peru to Hastings, Nebraska, and in 1913 to Crete, Nebraska, where I graduated from high school in 1917. In 1921, I graduated from Duane College with the degree of A.B. In 1923, I received the A.M. degree from the University of Nebraska, and in 1927, I was awarded the Ph.D. degree in Education from the University of Chicago. I served on the faculties of the University of Nebraska, the University of North Carolina, the Ohio State University and the University of Chicago. In 1953, I was appointed Director of the Center for Advanced Study in the Behavioral Sciences, which the Ford Foundation established on land leased from Stanford University. In 1967, I reached retirement age and since then have been a visiting scholar at a number of universities in the U.S. and abroad.

My expertise is in learning and instruction, curriculum development and educational evaluation. My best-known publication is Basic Principles of Curriculum and Instruction. The eight year study is the project which produced most significant educational generalizations. The development of the National Assessment of Educational Progress is the contribution of most current interest.

My mentors were: Herbert Bennett, chairman of secondary education at the University of Nebraska; Charles H. Judd, Chairman of the Department of Education at the University of Chicago; and W. W. Chambers, director of the Bureau of Educational Research, Ohio State University.

Currently, I am a part-time faculty member of the University of Massachusetts in Amherst, working with the faculties of the University and eleven school districts -- a coalition for School Improvement.

EDUCATIONAL CONCERNS

My philosophy is an effort to guide educational activities to help young people learn to be constructive citizens in a democratic society, able to think for themselves, identify and solve problems they encounter, develop their own unique talents and be engaged in learning throughout their lives.

My interest in the needs of children developed because my mother bore eight children. I was the sixth and was expected to participate in the care of my younger siblings. I liked this responsibility and actively sought to understand what children needed. I have seen many changes in the lives of children since 1902, primarily because of the increasing breakdown in the nuclear family and the resulting separation of generations. I find fewer children have learned to take responsibility for others, and fewer children are obtaining guidance from the home. Increasingly, children are receiving less personal attention from persons who care about them.

Qualities teachers and parents should strive for, in the child's developing years, include helping the child explore wider environments and encouraging the child to reflect upon and evaluate his or her experiences so as to gain a broader and deeper understanding of others. Teachers and parents should also help the child learn to work with others in activities focused on the general welfare, particularly the welfare of children. The child should be encouraged to learn to use the works of scholars in gaining advice, rather than follow the superficial ideas of TV, the mass media and the "man on the street." The child should be guided to discover the satisfaction and joy of gaining new understanding by responding emotionally to works of art and of music.

Education's greatest allies are parents and other persons in the community who care about children. Its greatest enemies are cultures and individuals who seek material rewards ahead of human welfare and persons who are indifferent to the human condition. The agent of socialization that has the greatest potential for affecting the lives of children differs with the child's age. Young children are more deeply affected by the home and school, the most important influences in their development. For adolescents, the peer group and attractive adults who serve as role models, whom the adolescents seek to emulate, are most important.

The most influential leaders in the lives of children are viewed differently by children and adults. The persons adults consider leaders are not necessarily persons children consider leaders. Young children commonly identify as leaders persons they know and admire - usually a parent, a teacher, a principal, a man in the candy store or another vendor who listens to them and seems to care. It could be the school janitor, etc. As children get older, they often consider an attractive TV artist as a leader, as well as adults and peers that they know. Teachers and parents need to help children identify persons thay they can see as constructive leaders.

Historical leaders of the past that I credit with changing the lives of children in a significantly positive manner are persons who influence adult views, rather than persons viewed as leaders by children. Francis W. Parker, superintendent of the public schools in Quincy, Massachusetts, secured the attention of adults of goodwill when he stated: "Education frees the human spirit." Prior to that time, education was viewed generally as a process of inducting children into adulthood, like breaking in a horse. Children were to be disciplined to be obedient and become like adults. John Dewey developed Parker's view into a comprehensive philosophy and a psychology of learning. Ella Flagg Young, superintendent of the Chicago public schools, received her doctorate from John Dewey and sought to change the Chicago schools into more humane institutions.

My role as a change agent for children is exercised in the following manner: as an educational psychologist working with teachers and principals on the problems they encounter in the fields of curriculum and evaluation, I discuss with them the meaning of their activities, especially as they influence the child's development. These discussions are followed by their efforts to improve their work in order to help children develop as intelligent, outgoing, responsible persons. These efforts are examined and discussed as we work together, seeking to make continuous improvement.

In regard to areas in which public/private schools are performing well or not performing well in meeting the needs of children, I must state that the schools in America are not all alike. Not only are there wide variations among the 26,000 school districts in the ethnic, economic and social backgrounds of the families among the school districts, but within the same city, the variations in the problems encountered, the resources available and the effectiveness of the schools in helping children learn is large. If one is concerned with improving the actual experiences of children, one must focus on the particular school and

172

work with the teachers and parents there. In my travels about the United States, I find excellent schools and very poor schools and mediocre schools. One cannot answer accurately the question of what schools in general are accomplishing, but one can answer in terms of particular schools or particular types of schools.

The change I feel is most needed for children in both home and school is the evidence that parents and teachers really care about their children and encourage them to learn what schools are expected to help them learn. Impersonal atmosphere and treating children as a mass, rather than showing interest in them as individuals, are common dangers in school and community. Adults who care and share constructive experiences with children are greatly needed.

The role of technology in the lives of children should be a means of carrying on activities, not an end. Modern technology is used by children as well as adults in many activities, and we need periodically to review their effects. As an example, the automobile was developed to aid transportation, but it has become an end in itself. Many people love their autos and use them when they are not needed, as in going 1/4 mile to a shop, whereas they need more exercise in walking than most people now get.

The technology that probably influences children most is the television. Studies of television viewing by children indicate that TV distracts children from educational activities by furnishing alternative entertainment. The average child from 10 to 14 years of age is forced to spend much more time watching TV than the child spends in school. There are technologies that may be helpful to a teacher in assisting with activities which the teacher has difficulty carrying on, but the danger is that we become admirers and lovers of the technology rather than thoughtful users.

In his 1981 address as President of the American Association for the Advancement of Science, Kenneth Boulding pointed out that one cannot predict accurately the future of human beings. He said, "When people discover that conditions are becoming intolerable, they do something about it." Human beings have a considerable control over their society and their social institutions. We can identify serious current problems, but when the public will become sufficiently aroused to do something about them, is not predictable. Our society, its families and schools will not go down the drain, but we cannot foresee now how they will be renewed.

SELECTED PUBLICATION BIBLIOGRAPHY

Tyler, Ralph W., and Waples, Douglas. Research Methods and Teachers' Problems: A Manual for Systematic Studies of Classroom Procedure. New York: Macmillan Co., 1930.

Tyler, Ralph W. Constructing Achievement Tests. Columbus: Bureau of Educational Research, Ohio State University, 1934.

Smith, Eugene R.; Tyler, Ralph W.; and the Evaluation Staff. Appraising and Recording Student Progress: Evaluation, Records and Reports in the Thirty Schools. Progressive Education Association, Commission on the Relation of School and College, Adventure in American Education, Vol. 3. New York: Harper & Brothers, 1942.

Tyler, Ralph W. Basic Principles of Curriculum and Instruction. Chicago: University of Chicago Press, 1949.

Tyler, Ralph W. Perspectives on American Education: Reflections on the Past...Challenges for the Future. Chicago: Science Research Associates, 1976.

Kolodziey, Helen M., comp. Ralph W. Tyler: A Bibliography: 1929-1986. Washington, D. C.: National Foundation for the Improvement of Education, 1986. ED 272 496; distributed by Educational Resources Information Center Document Reproduction Service, Alexandria, Virginia 22304.

Barry J. Wadsworth

AUTOBIOGRAPHICAL SKETCH OF
BARRY WADSWORTH

My educational background includes having been a student at the West Side School in Cold Spring Harbor on Long Island, which was a 3-room schoolhouse at the time I was there. My bachelor and masters degree are both from the State University of New York at Oswego (in education) and my doctoral degree is from the State University of New York at Albany (Educational Psychology and Statistics). In adddition, I had the good forutne to study learning disorders for several months with Newell Kephart at the Glen Haven Achievement Center in Fort Collins, Colorado.

My educational expertise, so to speak, is in educational psychology in general and learning disorders. I have been very interested in developmental theory and, in particular, Piaget's theory and its implications for education. Secondary but important areas of interest are psychological and educational testing and quantitative reasoning.

I suppose my major contributions to education have been the two books I have published: <u>Piaget's Theory of Cognitive and Affective Development</u> (1971, 1979, 1984), which is going into the 4th revision, and <u>Piaget for the Classroom Teacher</u> (1978). I like to think my writing has made Piaget's work more accessible to some readers.

My mentors have been Eva Risley Clark, our teacher at the West Side School, and Jean Piaget. In my college work, there were several professors who continue to influence my work including Jim Marcuso at Albany and Newell Kephart at Glen Haven.

The first 7 years of my professional career, I was a 7th grade teacher in a self-contained classroom on Long Island. Currently, I am a Professor of Psychology and Education and director of the teacher preparation program at Mount Holyoke College in South Hadley, Massachusetts. I am involved in teaching psychology courses and teacher preparation courses in education. I have also recently finished a nine year stint as a member of the South Hadley School Committee.

CAN THE PAST INFORM THE PRESENT?

During the summer prior to my year in 5th grade, shortly after World War II, my family moved across Long Island from Baldwin to Cold Spring Harbor, a small, former whaling village on the North Shore. My sister, brother and I were enrolled in the West Side School in Cold Spring Harbor, which at the time was a 3-room schoolhouse. I was in the upper level which was composed of grades 5-8. There were usually 20-25 children in the 4 grades during any one year. The teacher was Eva Risley Clark. She was also the "principal" and had to do just about everything. The backgrounds of children in the class were economically quite diverse. Many children came from local "estates" - either children of the owners or children of those who worked in the estate. There was 1 child in the class who was black and one boy who was an immigrant from Germany and spoke no English.

From where I sit now, I look back upon my 3 years in the West Side School as a highlight of my educational experience. It was a very good school! I frequently use those years as one frame against which to compare and judge what I encounter now in education. There were principles at work which I can't ignore.

Why was this situation in that 3-room school so good? There were 4 "grade levels" of students in one class. The teacher had no adult assistance and so much responsibility. Mrs. Clark had to contend with a variety of demands which many teachers today would consider burdensome and necessarily unmanageable. In retrospect, I believe that many of the seeming "burdens" were indeed "virutes" which helped to make the school as good as it was.

First of all, Mrs. Clark had virtually all the responsibility for the school and its functioning. She had to see that everything got done and still "teach" a group of 25 diverse students. The virtue here was that Mrs. Clark had a great deal of <u>autonomy</u> in what she did and how she did it. The things that went well were in part her doing. The things that went less well were also in part of her doing. She had ownership, control, freedom, responsibility -- autonomy and investment. Its successes were her successes.

How did she deal with 4 grade levels in one classroom? Clearly a conventional <u>structure</u> was not possible. The opening period in each day was a time to write. Everyone was always writing a story or paper of some sort. Periodically, Mrs. Clark would check our writing. It was o.k. for other students to read your story and make suggestions. This happened a lot. The last portion of the day was spent assembled in the library corner of our room, where a student and Mrs. Clark would read a student's story to all. She stopped occasionally to comment on some aspect of the writing she thought was important.

For arithmetic, each student had a grade level workbook/textbook for whatever grade level they were working at. Students worked on their text and workbook and took the periodic quizzes which occurred. Periodically, there were whole class discussions of particular mathematical concepts. Mrs. Clark visited with every student every couple of days to check how they were doing and always corrected quizzes herself. If you were having problems understanding something, you sought out Mrs. Clark, if she didn't spot a problem first. If Mrs. Clark was busy when you needed her, you would go to another student in the class and get help. This was the expected and accepted procedure. Everyone did it. Working with other students happened a lot. Most students made their way through more than one grade level text/workbook a year. Many students completed algebra during their stay. Some went further.

When we had an English Class, 5, 6, 7 and 8th grade students were all part of the same class. There were usually no 5th grade English or 8th grade English except when special problems were spotted. Typically, everyone got the same English lesson. I don't think we were all expected to learn everything to the same degree but to take away from it what we could. After 4 years, students knew quite a bit. History involved a lot of reading and project work. We were always reading and writing about topics in history and geography. Periodically, Mrs. Clark would ask us to share our work with the class. Occasionally, the teacher lectured or talked to us about some general principle.

Mrs. Clark didn't like science. I believe she considered herself totally inept in this area. Since she thought hands-on science work was important, Mrs. Clark imported a retired biologist, Mrs. Demerest, to handle the hands-on science work. In the basement of our building, there was a large storage-like room. Mrs. Demerest lined the walls with shelves and proceeded to fill the shelves with all orders of "junk" she collected and considered worthy of scientific curiosity. These included: stuffed birds, shell collections, leaf collections, butterfly and bug collections, an old electric motor, varieties of bottles and jars, etc., etc., etc. It seemed to us, everything imaginable was in that room. Part of science was getting involved with some of these materials, reading about related things, etc. <u>Spontaneous interests</u> were nurtured. I remember some boys who disassembled an electric motor after having it turn all sorts of things. They marveled over the inner arrangements. They proceeded to try to reassemble the motor. Needless to say, Mrs. Demerest was needed to help wrap up this project. At one point, the class was called together, and for an hour, the boys explained what they had done. There was a lot of discussion about motors, electricity, etc. These group sessions about projects occurred regularly.

We also did a lot of science projects outside when the weather permitted. While Mrs. Clark seemed to actively avoid hands-on science, she was not above seizing interesting opportunities. One morning, a parent called Mrs. Clark and reported there was a whale beached by a receding tide at a nearby harbor.

> When she heard about the stranded whale she immediately arranged for a bus, and within an hour, the whole school (about sixty children and three teachers) saw a whale: a real, live, fullblown whale sitting (and suffering, I am certain) on a beach. Unfortunate as the whale's condition was, it provided a feast for the eyes. We looked at it; we listened to it; we went up to it to touch it (it could not move much); we ran away from it when it opened its massive mouth; we threw water on it; we made faces at it -- we did all sorts of things. From that day on, we all knew exactly what a whale was! I do not remember what we were studying in class the week before our whale, but I know we did a lot of things relating to whales the week after. We talked about whales, we drew pictures of whales. We learned a lot about whales by being <u>active</u>, and the activity gave more <u>meaning</u> to what we later read and heard. (Wadsworth, 1978, pp. 54-55.)

We didn't have a lot of tests (except in arithmetic), though we certainly produced a lot of written work which was always carefully discussed with us. One had the sense that Mrs. Clark knew how each student was progressing in everything. If we were having trouble with something, she helped us herself or got another student to help us. For two years, we didn't have any report cards or formal communication to parents. Sometimes there was a phone call, a written note or visit with a parent. My third year, every parent got a written note.

My family moved again at the end of my 7th grade year. I do

recall that when the 8th graders went off to high school in the neighboring community's high school, the reports on their academic performance were uniformly favorable. They all seemed to do well, even the students who we considered not the brightest in our group.

By many conventional educational criteria, this was an <u>inefficient</u> school. One teacher for 4 grade levels; no clear grade levels; no uniform tightly adhered-to curriculum by grade levels; none of the amenities that the superior resources of large school systems bring to education.

But things happened in this seemingly "inefficient" school which were educationally very sound. Was it just the teacher? I think not. Mrs. Clark <u>was</u> very good. But one of the reasons why she was effective and why students were uniformly productive, was the structure underlying that particular school which permitted (and maybe demanded) a variety of practices considered by some criteria to be "inefficient". I would argue that these practices resulted in students graduating who were educated for their level, had positive attitudes about themselves as learners and about schools and teachers.

This school worked very well. It had a "family" atmosphere; students knew others cared for them, and there was a lot of necessary cooperation. The teachers had considerable autonomy. The students had considerable autonomy. Everyone respected everyone else. There were rules -- and we "obeyed" them because we knew the teacher cared about us, and we respected and valued that.

The curriculum seemed "loose" and, at times, non-existent -- certainly not the overarching priority. But I now know that Mrs. Clark had a plan and had a good sense of where we all were most of the time. She got to know her students very, very well, having them for so many years. I do think this helped her to know and understand us and permitted her to feel more clearly that our accomplishments were her accomplishments as well -- which, of course, they were.

Mrs. Clark believed all kids could learn. She believed this of me, the black girl in our class and the boy who came from Germany with no spoken English.

Romanticism? I think not. This was a real school, and it was noteable because of the uniformly positive contribution it made to children's development as learners and healthy individuals. We

180

cannot, nor should, return to the 3-room schoolhouses. We should not overlook or dismiss the best educational principles found in them. Maybe having a teacher work with the same group of students for several years is possible and isn't an "inefficient" idea. Maybe having "loose" or more flexible curriculum demands and more autonomy for teachers to work with children they know can improve learning and affective outcomes. It is important that the people in school systems care. Maybe the environments we create effect all these things.

REFERENCES

Wadsworth, Barry. Piaget for the Classroom Teacher. New York: Longman, 1978.

PUBLICATION BIBLIOGRAPHY

BOOKS:

Wadsworth, Piaget's Theory of Cognitive Development: an introduction for students of psychology and education, New York: David McKay Co., 1971.

Wadsworth, Piaget for the Classroom Teacher, New York: Longman, 1978.

Wadsworth, Piaget's Theory of Cognitive Development: an introduction for students of psychology and education, 2nd edition, New York: Longman, 1979.

Wadsworth, Piaget's Theory of Cognitive and Affective Development, New York: Longman, 1984.

OTHER PUBLICATIONS:

Wadsworth, Runte, and Tookey, Values of Seminarians and Novices, Psych. Reports, 23, 870, 1968.

Wadsworth, The Origins of Intellect: Piaget's Theory, Phillips, J., The Record, 71, (3), 1970; a review.

Wadsworth and Nord, the effects of interspersed questions on learning from written materials in elementary school children and college students. Research in Education, June, 1971.

Wadsworth, Comparison of the Theoretical Constructs of Piaget and Kephart, "Exceptional Child Education Abstracts", Vol. 8, No. 1, Spring, 1976.

Wadsworth, "Piaget's concept of adaptation and its value to educators". In: Piagetian Theory and the Helping Professions (8th Annual Piagetian Conference Proceedings), Los Angeles, University of Southern California, 1979.

181

Wadsworth, Review of Gallagher and Easley, Knowledge and Development, Vol. 2, Journal of Moral Development, 1979.

Wadsworth, Misinterpretations of Piaget's Theory, Impact on Curriculum Improvement, Vol. 16, No. 2, 1981.

WORKS IN PROGRESS:

Preparation of a book dealing with adolescent cognitive development and the application of developmental concepts to teaching at the middle school and high school levels.

Development and standardization of an assessment procedure for assessing cognitive development (using Piagetian developmental procedures) in children from ages 4 through 16.

Revision of Piaget's Theory of Cognitive and Affective Development Class.

Selma Wassermann

AUTOBIOGRAPHICAL SKETCH OF
SELMA WASSERMANN

Selma Wassermann is currently Professor of Education at Simon Fraser University.

In reflecting on my life, those who I credit with teaching me much include:

Louis E. Raths -- my main man; a great thinker, a great teacher, a great humanitarian. He taught me about thinking, and valuing, and emotional needs, and power. He opened my eyes to the impact of teacher-student interactions on student learning.

Sylvia Ashton-Warner -- my creative guru. A creative genius, she taught me to "open my creative vent" and to write. She "supplied the conditions" for me to develop as a writer.

Ed Lipinski, M.D. -- chief shrink at Simon Fraser University. He took me under his wing and allowed me to learn from him, in a long-term clinical practicum, about how people grow therapeutically well, and crooked. He taught me about openness and defensiveness and helped me to gain much insight into self.

My responsiblities at Simon Fraser are many. I am a teacher first; the type that Donald Schon would call "Reflective Practitioner." I am happiest when I am in the process of developing new programs and implementing them in classroom practice. New programs that are in operation under my supervision include:

*Critical Incidents in Teaching: The Teacher as Decision-Maker.

*Curriculum Studies: Teaching for Thinking.

New program on the drawing boards include:

*Teacher Education by the Case Method (a new pre-service training program using the case method and the instructional model, Play-Debrief-Replay, as a teaching vehicle).

What I do as an extension of my work at SFU includes promoting teaching for thinking in inservice work in schools across the province, Canada and the states. Research activities are heavily based in teaching for thinking in-school work.

If asked what I'm good at, my response would be teaching. I think I am a very good teacher, who has learned that teaching is very much more than giving an inspirational lecture. I keep studying the act of teaching, trying to improve my skills, so that my students are consistently enabled. I think that is the key to successful teaching.

Writing is another area I feel good about. I think I am a capable writer -- who can communicate ideas as well as affect, in ways that are challenging as well as interesting. Additionally, program development is an area of expertise for me. I have learned that programs are much more than a string of courses put together. I'm very good at putting together programs that are based in a theoretical framework, that have clearly articulated goals, and in which teaching and other educational experiences within the program all work in harmony toward the realization of the program's goals.

The arenas in which I am now stirring the mud around include:
Teaching for thinking: my first love.
The teacher as decision-maker.
Case study approach to teacher education.
Play-Debrief-Replay: an instructional model that enables pupils to grow and learn.

Educational background:
Public school education in Brooklyn, New York.
Undergraduate work and teacher training at C.C.N.Y.
Master's Degree in Reading with Jeanne Chall and Florence Roswell, also at C.C.N.Y.
Doctorate at New York University in Curriculum and Instruction with Louis E. Raths as my main mentor.

Publications of which I am most proud:
Teaching For Thinking: Theory, Strategies and Activities For the Classroom. Louis E. Raths, Selma Wassermann, Arthur Jonas and Arnold Rothstein (second edition). NY: Teachers College Press, 1986.

Put Some Thinking In Your Classroom. Selma Wassermann. San Diego: Coronado, 1978.

Teaching Elementary Science: Who's Afraid of Spiders? Selma Wassermann & George Ivany. NY: Harper & Row, 1988.

The Battle of the Bulge (a cookbook!). Selma Wassermann. Vancouver: Tarragon Books, 1986.

The Thinking and Learning Programs. Selma Wassermann. Four boxes of classroom materials that enable children (grades 3, 4, 5, & 6) to think at higher cognitive levels. San Diego:

Coronado, 1984.

And several of the more than 75 journal articles that have appeared under my name in the last 25 years.

LEARNING TO TEACH

It was not an easy decision to take a leave of absence from university teaching to return to an elementary classroom. Not only was such an action not understood by colleagues, it was the cause of much mirth. Having made good one's escape into the rarefied environs of the "halls of ivy", what could one possibly hope to gain by a return to the swampy lowlands of the public schools?

I was not prepared for the heat of September in that Marin County classroom where I was to lose my innocence -- me, a veteran teacher with nearly 20 years of "on the line" experience at that time. I didn't remember classrooms being so small. We were crowded into it, 26 sweating strangers. The honeymoon period was quick; after two days, all semblance of politeness evaporated and unbridled aggression surfaced with unrelenting vigor. Upon reflection, I had to concede that these fifth and sixth graders were by far the most socially unattractive pupils I'd ever met.

The tallest and the most gentle of them was Gary. A grade 6 student, he towered above most of the other boys by as much as two feet. Gentle in the classroom, he was a tiger on the sports field. Watching him shoot baskets, one could admire his strength, his skill, his grace and think, "This boy could be a star." In the classroom, he was the butt of children's grim and devastating put-downs. Gary's overall academic work was only marginal, but where he really succeeded in distinguishing himself as an utter failure was in math. While he could add two plus two, he was in trouble if you increased the amount of either numeral by one digit. Two plus three was entirely outside his reach, and any arithmetic worksheet that called on his ability to add and subtract whole numbers was returned with the most extraordinary hodgepodge of incorrect responses that I had ever seen. There was no clear, discernible pattern to his errors -- and I could not even distill, from

186

intensive examination of his work, a workable diagnosis. It was tempting to think of brain damage -- of some numerary retardation. Had some of his math brain cells been wiped out in a prenatal or early childhood truma?

His mother lost no time in coming up for a visit. She brought with her the diagnostic assessments of a local clinic, where a group of professionals served the community by testing and evaluating young children's mental competence. I read that Gary's I.Q. was 80, and he could read and comprehend at about 4th grade level. No assessment had been made of his mathematical functioning. Mrs. Newhouse was frightened. Would this new teacher (me) be sympathetic to the problems of her only son? Would there be some way to help him learn? Should she believe what these imposing, formally constructed and expensive letters of assessment told her? The boys in his peer group continued to villify him. "Retard" was the argot of the day; they used the term as warriors used swords to maim and destroy.

I pulled out my bag of good teaching strategies and borrowed from the primary grade teacher a sack of cuisenaire rods. Simple, eh? If Gary was having trouble figuring out sums, then obviously he needed to work "hands on" with manipulatives so that he would "uncork" his cognitive block, grow in his conceptual understanding and get his sums correct. I gave Gary the sack of rods, a worksheet of simple addition examples and some initial instruction in how to use the rods as an aid in calculation. He took the rods silently; and I thought I detected a look on his face that told me a story, but I couldn't read it. The other students worked on fractions. When Gary turned in his arithmetic worksheet, the familiar hodgepodge of answers that made no sense were all in place. I hadn't noticed that he had quietly dispatched the rods to the innermost reaches of his desk. Three days, three rod-instruction periods and three worksheets later, we were still at square one. Gary, however, moved from grudging acceptance of this work to open hostility. "No wonder," I thought. "He thinks his teacher is a turkey. I can't help him either."

On Monday I decided I'd give it one more try.

"Hey, Gar, take out the rods and let's do some math."

Slowly, as though he were swimming through glue, he began to extract the bag of rods from his desk. I pulled a chair over to him and got a good look at the cold, hard face. It didn't take many questions to find out the trouble. Cuisenaire rods were for babies. I had publicly humiliated him with my choice of "hands on" materials. Never mind that we used them at the university and that college students found them wonderful tools. Everyone at this school KNEW they were only used in the primary grades. Why didn't I just put a dunce cap on his head and be done with it! Numb with shame, I took the sack of rods from Gary and retreated to a neutral corner where I could assess my losses.

It was a two-martini day by the time I got home and rethought the Gary situation. If rods were "for babies", I had to find some other manipulatives that would be more appropriate. They needed not just to help him conceptualize numbers but to restore his dignity. I decided on money.

I put together a bag of coins -- about five dollars worth, in pennies, nickels, dimes and quarters -- and told Gary that this would be his bag of money. "Gary's money," the other kids called it. No one could say that these manipulatives were for babies. He began to use the money as counters. Each day, he and I would put together a group of 10 arithmetic examples requiring him to add and subtract money. At the end of the day, he'd turn his worksheet into my "In File" for marking.

His pattern of "correct" responses was fairly consistent -- usually three or four correct out of ten, with five correct a major event. If there was a consistency about his low score, there was no discernible consistency to his patterns of errors. Working with him, one-on-one, a regular intervention, did not increase his ability to compute in any significant way. In the evenings, at the dining room table where I read students' work with my after-dinner coffee, I tried to think of what I might write on Gary's paper that would not demean him further, that would not destroy the remaining vestiges of confidence he had in himself. Yet I could not be false and write that his paper was "good work" because that, to me, would have been the ultimate betrayal. He would never have any reason to trust me again. Even "You are trying" seemed a reproach. I could not think of something to write that would be honest -- as well as supportive, encouraging and validating.

In a move that I never learned in any education course, I picked up my gum eraser and rubbed out a few incorrect digits in Gary's answers. Deviously, I selected a matching pencil, forged his handwriting, and put the correct digits in the correct spaces. Would he know? Would he remember the answers he had put down? Would such a lying, cheating maneuver doom us both? I poured a shot of brandy into my coffee cup, picked up my blue pencil and wrote, "Hey, Gary. Eight correct today! You are really making some big improvement in your work." I downed the brandy in a single gulp.

We played out this scenario for the next few months. Gary, despite extensive one-on-one instruction, practice with his bag of manipulatives and math worksheets, never learned to master computation with increased accuracy. I continued each evening to erase and change his incorrect answers so that I could return his paper with a response that validated Gary-as-a-person. Until now, I have never told any of this to a soul.

In the early days of spring, three boys from another class came into the after-schol disarray of my classroom to "hang out" and to talk with some of my "hangers-on." I heard them rapping from where I was putting together a photo display for the bulletin board.

"Who's the dumbest kid in your class?" one of them asked. Larry looked up from what he was doing and looked over at Mark, who liked me to call him Bob, and said, shrugging his shoulders, "I don't know."

It would be nice if the story had a happy ending. But the truth is, I left Marin County at the end of the school year and returned to my perch in the faculty of Education, at the very top of Burnaby Mountain -- lest we forget that we are the elite. I lost touch with Gary altogether. Did he ever get through high school with any shred of his self-worth intact -- even though he could not do his numbers? Is self-worth a reasonable price to pay for the inability to sum? Maybe a college coach picked him up, got him a basketball scholarship and gave him a free ride through the academic requirements. Never mind. Now I could concentrate on training teachers, telling them what they ought to be doing in their classrooms.

PUBLICATION BIBLIOGRAPHY

BOOKS:

Selma Wassermann and J. W. George Ivany, Teaching Elementary Science: Who's Afraid of Spiders? New York: Harper & Row, 1987 (in press).

Louis Raths, Selma Wassermann, Arthur Jonas and Arnold Rothstein, Teaching for Thinking: Theory, Strategies and Activities for the Classroom. New York: Teachers College Press, 1986.

Selma Wassermann, Put Some Thinking in Your Classroom. San Diego, Coronado, 1978.

Selma Wassermann, A Guide to the Improvement of Reading and Thinking. Chicago: Benefic Press, 1967.

Louis Raths, Selma Wassermann, Arthur Jonas and Arnold Rothstein, Teaching for Thinking: Theory and Application. Columbus, O.: Merrill, 1966.

JOURNAL ARTICLES:

Selma Wassermann, "Schools Are for Thinking: The Story of the Abbotsford Project," Canadian School Executive, September, 1987.

Selma Wassermann, "Training Teachers to Develop Classroom Competence: We Have No Easy Answers," Childhood Education, May/June, 1987.

Selma Wassermann, "Teaching Strategies: Enabling Children to Develop Personal Power Through Building Self Respect," Childhood Education, April, 1987.

Selma Wassermann, "Teaching For Thinking: Louis E. Raths Revisited." Phi Delta Kappan, February, 1987.

Selma Wassermann, "Teaching for Thinking: What Can the Principal Do?" Elementary Principal, January, 1987.

Selma Wassermann, "Teaching for Thinking: The Role of the Educational Leader," Canadian School Executive. June, 1986.

Selma Wassermann, "The Play," Teaching and Learning. Fall, 1986.

Selma Wassermann, "Beliefs and Personal Power: The Difference Between a Chairperson and a Charperson IS How She Behaves." College Teaching. Spring, 1986.

Selma Wassermann, "Teaching Strategies: Developing Personal Power." Childhood Education, December, 1986.

Selma Wassermann, "Growing Teachers in the Computer Age." Educational Digest, March, 1986.

Selma Wassermann, "What Can Schools Become?" Reprinted from Phi Delta Kappan. Education, Spring, 1986.

Selma Wassermann, "Even Teachers Get the Blues: Helping Teachers to Help Kids Learn." Childhood Education, September/October, 1985.

Selma Wassermann. "What Can Schools Become? Is There Life After Pac-Man?" Phi Delta Kappan, June, 1984.

Selma Wassermann, "Promoting Thinking in Your Classroom II: Our Means Are Inconsistent With Our Ends." Childhood Education, March/April, 1984.

Selma Wassermann, "Dear Sr. Buonarotti," Improving College and University Teaching. Fall, 1984.

Selma Wassermann, "The Gifted Can't Weigh That Giraffe." Reprinted from Phi Delta Kappan in the Metropolitan West Regional Committee for Talented Children Report, New South Wales, Australia, 1984.

Selma Wassermann, "The Gifted Can't Weigh That Giraffe." The New York Times, November 15, 1981, and reprinted in the following: Phi Delta Kappan, May, 1982; SFU Week, January, 1982, and others.

Selma Wassermann, "Interacting With Your Students," Childhood Education, May/June, 1982.

Selma Wassermann and Catherine Stanbrook, "Inverse Tutoring," Phi Delta Kappan, March, 1981.

Selma Wassermann and Wallace Eggert, "Profiles of Teaching Competency," Eric Clearinghouse on Teacher Education, Spring, 1981. (reprinted)

Selma Wassermann, "Teaching the Gifted," Roeper Review, September, 1981.

Selma Wassermann and Wallace Eggert, "Profiles of Teaching Competency," Washington, D. C.: Research in Education, March, 1981.

Selma Wassermann, "The Harpsichord Theory of Teacher Education," Teacher Education, October, 1980.

Selma Wassermann, 'Helping Relationships in the Classroom," Special Education in Canada, Vol. 53, January, 1979.

Selma Wassermann, "The Teacher As Curriculum Maker," Washington, D. C.: Association for Childhood Education International, Success-in-Teaching Series, November, 1979. (Reprinted from article in Childhood Education.)

Selma Wassermann, "Evaluation and the Emperor's New Clothes," Childhood Education, April/May, 1979.

Selma Wassermann, "Key Vocabulary: Impact on Beginning Reading," Young Children, May, 1978.

Selma Wassermann, "They Said It Couldn't Be Done," Canadian Journal of Education, Volume III, No. 1, 1978.

Selma Wassermann and Wallace Eggert, "Profiles of Teaching Competency: A Way of Looking at Classroom Teaching Performance," E + M Newsletter, OISE Educational Evaluation Centre, No. 29, February, 1978 (reprinted from Canadian Journal of Education).

Selma Wassermann, 'My Friend Connie," Phi Delta Kappan, December, 1977.

Selma Wassermann, "The Teacher As A Decision-Maker," Teacher Education, Spring, 1976.

Selma Wassermann, "The Organic Classroom: The Story of the Vancouver Project," Phi Delta Kappan, September, 1976.

Selma Wassermann, "The Teacher As A Curriculum Maker," Childhood Education, March, 1976.

Selma Wassermann and Wallace Eggert, "Profiles of Teaching Competency: A Way of Looking at Classroom Teaching Performance," Canadian Journal of Education, Volume 1, No. 1, January, 1976.

Selma Wassermann, "The Integrated Day in Teacher Education, or Putting Your Money Where Your Mouth Is," Childhood Education, April, 1973.

Selma Wassermann, "Aspen Mornings with Sylvia Ashton-Warner," Childhood Education, April, 1972.

Selma Wassermann, "What Do the Students Say?" Monday Morning, January, 1972.

Slema Wassermann, "Inhumanities in the Classroom," Impact, 1968.

Selma Wassermann, "Strapping: Educational Remnant from the Middle Ages," B. C. Teacher, 1967.

Selma Wassermann, "Thinking: Theory and Proctices," Focus, 1966.

CHAPTERS:

Selma Wassermann, "How I Taught Myself How to Teach," in Teaching by the Case Method. 2nd edition, R. C. Christensen, editor. Cambridge: Harvard Graduate School of Business Administratin, 1986.

Selma Wassermann, "The Gifted Can't Weigh That Giraffe," in <u>Teaching by the Case Method</u>. 2nd edition, R. C. Christensen, editor. Cambridge: Harvard Graduate School of Business Administration, 1986.

Selma Wassermann, "The Gifted Can't Weigh That Giraffe," in <u>Teaching by the Case Method</u>. 2nd edition, R. C. Christensen, editor. Cambridge: Harvard Graduate School of Business Administration, 1986. (Reprinted from the <u>New York Times</u>.)

Selma Wassermann, "What Can Schools Become? Is There Life After Pac-Man?" in <u>Elementary Education</u>, J. Michael Palardy, editor. New York: University Press of America, 1986. (Reprinted from <u>Kappan</u>.)

Selma Wassermann, "Curriculum Reform and Classroom Realities: Henny Penny, the Sky is Falling," in <u>Curriculum Canada</u>, edited by Richard Butt, John Olson, Jaques Daignault. Vancouver: Centre for the Study of Curriculum and Instruction, University of British Columbia, 1983.

Selma Wassermann, "Profile of Teacher Behavior," in <u>Education</u>, edited by Wilf Wees. Scarborough, Ontario: Gage Publishing Co., 1969.

David P. Weikart

AUTOBIOGRAPHICAL SKETCH OF
DAVID P. WEIKART

David P. Weikart is the President of High/Scope Educational Research Foundation, Ypsilanti, Michigan, a non-profit research development and training organization in education. He graduated from Oberlin College in 1953 and received his Ph.D. from the University of Michigan in Education and Psychology in 1966. Main areas of interest are early childhood care and education and non-formal adolescent learning.

EARLY INTERVENTION WORKS

My personal philosophy stems from my years of working with children, with their parents, and with their teachers. It is quite simple: adults have an obligation -- as individuals and as members of society -- to help the next generation reach its full potential. Adults can fulfill this obligation either directly, through program participation in implementation efforts, or indirectly, through involvement in social and political efforts at the local, state, and national level.

In my case, I have had the opportunity to serve children, both indirectly and directly, at the preschool and adolescent levels. The Ypsilanti Perry Preschool Project, now operated by the High/Scope Foundation, was initially established by me in the fall of 1962. I am also one of the founders of the High/Scope Summer Camp for Teenagers that has been serving talented teenagers since the summer of 1963. Thus, my opportunities to work directly with children through the summer program and indirectly through preschool research studies, program development, teacher training activities, parent programs, and program evaluation efforts were simultaneous occurrences. The extraordinary impact of the Perry Preschool Project has amazed me. We established the program with only one goal in mind: to encourage the Ypsilanti Public Schools to recognize the needs of young, disadvantaged children in the community. From my particular vantage point as director of Special Services, I could see that many of the older disadvantaged youth in the system were having a difficult time in school. To me, it was a foregone conclusion that their younger siblings would experience similar difficulties.

It semed to me that providing an intervention program for young children might help resolve the problems that would surely crop up later in their lives. There was nothing very glamorous or profound about this thinking -- simply a school system taking action to foster the healthy growth of its young students. It was a simple, straightforward approach to meeting a real need in our local community.

I think the research aspect of the Perry Preschool study is most responsible for its far-reaching influence. We did what few others at the time chose to do -- we decided to follow our participants in a carefully controlled manner and find out if there were any benefits in both the short-term and long-term that could be shown on an objective basis. We had a good program -- of that we were sure -- but we had no proof as to its efficacy. The research provided the proof we needed to illustrate the value of early childhood education.

Because of my strong research orientation, I believe that research must serve as a basis for planning the future of education and care for children. I recognize the inherent danger that research can be used ill-advisedly to prove narrow points while ignoring broader issues. Nevertheless, I believe research helps us set limits and keeps us honest in the sense of providing an objective sounding board for ideas and theories. Take for example, the question of how fast and early children should learn the alphabet. Research shows us that this is not the question we should be analyzing with regard to young children; instead, we should be studying when the alphabet might be of some use and how it can be incorporated in the broader goals of the child's development. Learning some artificial names of some marks on paper is of little intrinsic value to young children. We have to find ways to support learning as a meaningful experience for children so that they can make their knowledge a functional extension of themselves. Research should guide such efforts.

The lesson learned about the value of sound research does not just apply to education. The Perry Project also has helped us realize the broader economic and social benefits of early education: the reduction of social problems for the community at large and the economic savings that high quality early childhood education programs can achieve. Children who experience high quality early education appear to be more effective in society and less likely to be liabilities. To find that the committee for Economic Development used the High/Scope arguments in their campaign to encourage the business community to provide more child care and preschool programs is testimony to the effectiveness of our arguments. Additionally, state after state has used the High/Scope data to argue for investment in early childhood education as a way of improving the social chances of its citizens.

These outcomes give me a sense of both personal and professional satisfaction about the effectiveness of work begun almost 25 years ago. Yet, in the beginning, I had no inkling that our programs would have such a far-reaching impact. Perhaps it is because of this that today I firmly believe each of us must follow our personal and professional responsibilities as far as they take us -- we cannot shirk the responsibilities that come our way, or shrink from the opportunities that open up for us. My own experience is positive proof that the outcomes of small initial efforts, as pebbles in a pond, can have boundless effects.

Perhaps the most rewarding aspect of working in the education field is the feedback I receive from persons who have participated in our programs. Recently, for example, I was on an airplane flying back from Washington; as we were disembarking in Detroit, someone behind me called, "Dr. Weikart, Dr. Weikart." I turned around to see a well-dressed, familiar-looking young man working his way up the aisle. He turned out to be one of our summer camp "graduates" -- now a law clerk in the Supreme Court. He remembered me well, he said, and had fond memories of our many conversations. I remembered that he had been an eager participant in the camp program and had marked himself as a young man with substantial prospects. He told me that his camp experience had helped him learn how to broaden friendships and to develop his problem-solving skills. He felt that his camp experience had given him the courage to test out his emerging convictions. Clearly, he had used the camp experience in a profitable way.

While I cannot say that the High/Scope Camp created this talented and obviously successful young man, it appears to have contributed in a positive way to his development. This type of feedback from "graduates" of High/Scope programs is most gratifying and strengthens my resolve to continue to help the "next generation."

I have been fortunate in being able to put my philosophy into action through the establishment of the High/Scope Foundation, which I founded in 1970. A key aspect of the foundation's work is training adults to work effectively with children and adolescents. Another important Foundation effort has been the development and widespread implementation of the High/Scope Curriculum. We designed the curriculum so that as teachers gain an understanding of child growth and development they can devise their own program within the framework of the school or day care setting within which they are working. It is my very strong belief that educational programs should not be subject to some rigid formula of program instruction to the point where both the teacher's and the student's personal development and innovation are artificially constrained. Accordingly, the High/Scope Curriculum was developed to be flexible. It is really a methodology rather than a curriculum, and it is based on conceptual organization and philosophy rather than upon specific materials and didactic formats. It is a great pleasure for me to go into a school that is using the High/Scope methodology and find that the teachers have adapted it to their particular children and needs. I am still able to find the basic elements or our apporach in each classroom -- the plan-do-review sequence, child-initiated learning activity, and teacher support that is appropriate to each child's level of development. Thus, whether the language of the classroom is Spanish, Norwegian, Dutch, Arabic, or English, the High/Scope Curriculum is in action.

This leads me to the final point I wish to emphasize with regard to my basic philosophy of education: we must engage children in activities that are most comfortable and challenging for them, not for us; equally important, we must approach teachers in the same manner. We must focus on the true needs of both children and teachers rather than on artificial goals that require so much control and execution that real learning cannot occur. I believe strongly that to have happy, fulfilled children, we must have happy, fulfilled teachers -- the two go hand in hand. I therefore focus a great deal of effort on working with teachers. I want teachers to be satisfied with their work and to experience a sense of personal gratification with their own success. I want them to be happy with their peers as well, as they engage in a fruitful exchange of ideas, solutions, and suggestions. In practical terms, when I walk into a classroom I don't want a teacher to tell me, "Dave, this is your program, see if you approve." What I'm looking for is a teacher who says, "This is my program, and you can see how I've been able to apply the High/Scope methodology in my setting." When a teacher tells me this, I know that the children being served are in the best possible educational setting -- a setting that will help them become all that they can be. To put it more personally, I know that I am doing all that I can, in my way, to give members of the next generation a chance for a good life.

PUBLICATION BIBLIOGRAPHY

Weikart, D. P. (1967). Preschool Programs: Preliminary Findings. Journal of Special Education, 1, 163-181. Reprinted in Feather, B. and Ilsen, W. S. (Eds.). (1969). Children, psychology, and the schools. Glenview, Ill.: Scott, Foresman and Co.

Weikart, D. P. (1970). A comparative study of three preschool curricula. In Frost, J. (Ed.) Disadvantaged child, 2nd edition. New York: Houghton Mifflin. Reprinted in Lindgren, H. C. & Lindgren, F. (1971). Current readings in educational psychology, 2nd edition, New York, John Wiley. Reprinted in Handbook of Research on Equality of Educational Opportunity. (1973). New York: AMS Press, Inc.

Weikart, D. P. (1972). Relationship of curriculum, teaching, and learning in preschool education. In Stanley, J. C. (Ed.) Preschool programs for the disadvantaged: Five experimental approaches to early childhood education. Baltimore: John Hopkins Press.

Weikart, D P., & Banet, B. A. (1975). Model design problems in Follow Through. In Rivlin, A. M., & Timpane, M. (Eds.) Planned Variation: Should we give up or try harder? Washington, D. C.: The Brookings Institution.

Weikart, D. P. (1976). Preschool intervention for the disadvantaged child: A challenge for special education. In Spicker, H. H., Anastasiow, N. J., & Hodges, W. L. (Eds.) Children with special needs: Early development and education. Minneapolis: Leadership Training Institute/Special Education.

Weikart, D. P. (1979). Integrated Participation in the Process of Change. International Journal of Psychology. Nijmegen, Netherlands.

Weikart, D. P. (1981). Effects of Different Curricula in Early Childhood Intervention. Educational Evaluation and Policy Analysis, 3, 6, 25-34.

Weikart, D. P. (1981, Fall). Quality Preschool Education: A Wise Investment for the Schools. Principal, LVII, 8.

Weikart, D. P. (1984). Project Follow Through. International Encyclopedia of Education. Pergamon Press, Oxford, England.

Weikart, D. P. (1984, Winter). Changed Lives. American Educator, 8, 4. Condensed reprint in Prakken Publications (1985). The Education Digest, An Early Education Project That Changed Students' Lives, 32-34.

Berrueta-Clement, J. R., Schweinhart, L. J., Barnett, W. S., Epstein, A. S., & Weikart, D. P. (1984). Changed Lives: The Effects of the Perry Preschool Program on Youth Through Age 19. Monographs of the High/Scope Educational Research Foundation, No. 8.

Epstein, A. S., & Weikart, D. P. (1979). Longitudinal follow-up of the Ypsilanti Carnegie Infant Education Project. Monographs of the High/Scipe Educational Research Foundation, No. 6.

Hohmann, M., Banet, B., & Weikart, D. P. (1979). Young Children in Action: A Manual for Preschool Educators. Ypsilanti, MI: High/Scope Press.

Schweinhart, L. J., Weikart, D. P., & Larner, M. B., (1986). Consequences of three preschool curriculum models through age 15. Early Childhood Research Quarterly, 1(1), 15-45.

Burton L. White

AUTOBIOGRAPHICAL SKETCH OF
BURTON L. WHITE

Founder and Director of the Center for Parent Education, Dr. White is regarded as the country's foremost authority on the education of infants and toddlers, a subject he has been studying for almost 30 years. He was the director of the Harvard Preschool Project during its 13 years of existence, the first director of the Brookline Early Education Project, and was the senior consultant to Missouri's New Parents as Teachers Project.

Dr. White is the author of <u>The First Three Years of Life</u> and <u>Educating the Infant and Toddler</u>, as well as four major textbooks and numerous scholarly articles. He is also the host of a television series, "The First Three Years," produced by the Westinghouse Broadcasting Company.

BABIES AND EDUCATION

When I began my graduate career, I had no professional interest whatsoever in young children or babies. My focus back in the early 1950's was on why some people were so much more capable and decent than others. I had already concluded that my own enjoyment in life was directly tied to the quality of the people with whom I interacted. I wondered about the possibilities for helping people become more able and more caring. It was this simple humanistic interest that led me into the field of psychology, and before long, to the work of Abraham Maslow.

For the most part, study in the field of psychology didn't lead directly to practical approaches. On the whole, the field seemed more oriented in esoteric directions. There was a unanimous opinion within the field, however, that to understand how a particular adult functioned, one had to know in some detail the full life history of that person. Furthermore, there was general agreement that a person's environment and the experiences that resulted played a major role in determining the quality of the adult. In addition, it was generally accepted that the earlier the experiences, the more likely they were to have a profound effect on the long-term development of the person. These, then, were the principal reasons that led me to the study of the very young child.

My first research focus became the identification of the earliest abilities of people and the types of experiences that might be of significant influence in determining the quality of their development. Having come from the field of mechanical engineering (in which I obtained my first degree), I was considerably in awe of the difficulties of establishing reliable knowledge about the role of experience in the development of the child. I therefore concluded that I would probably spend my entire professional career trying to unravel the interrelationships among experiences and developing abilities in the first six months of a human's life. Fate, however, intervened.

After some eight years of research on the first six months of life, the dramatic increase in interest in preschool education signalled by the introduction of the Head Start project (1965) led to a quite remarkable opportunity for me. Along with the establishment of preschool educational programming for three to five-year-olds, 1965 saw the establishment of an intense research effort on the subject of preschool learning. On the basis of my work with very young infants, which by that time had received a fair amount of attention, the Harvard Graduate School of Education offered me the opportunity to study learning during the first six years of life while being provided with remarkably generous funding from the U. S. Office of Education and the Carnegie Corporation of New York (between $200,000 and $250,000 a year). I accepted the offer and rapidly recruited a reasearch staff of 17 people, all of whom were focused on one subject: How do you structure experiences in the first six years of life so as to help each child become the best developed and most decent six-year-old he/she could?

After a thorough examination of the literature on early development, we came to the conclusion that only a relatively small fraction of what needed to be known about that subject had indeed been established. We concluded that most of this theoretical work on early learning was inadequately supported by evidence, and we therefore were obliged to take a different track.

Our approach was comparatively simple. It was clear that some small fraction of all children develop into absolutely delightful six-year-olds, and each year saw more and more of them born and moving toward that admirable state. We decided to take a good hard look at how such a wonderful outcome happened under natural circumstances.

Making extensive use of repeated naturalistic observations, we developed a reasonably sound picture of what a wonderful six-year-old looked like. In the months that followed, we looked at five-year-olds, four-year-olds, and three-year-olds, and we found something quite surprising. Outstanding three-year-old children had usually developed the core attributes of everything that made the outstanding six-year-old special. This finding was of fundamental importance for our research, particularly in the case of families with little wealth or education. If we could learn how they were producing three-year-olds who had most of the basic attributes of outstanding six-year-olds, we would, in our judgment, be learning something of enormous importance.

Interestingly, and not merely coincidentally, experimental work in educational practice was coming to conclusions similar to our own. The experimentation in the Head Start venture was, at least to us, proving very clearly that it was quite a difficult undertaking to help a poorly developing three-year-old become a good or above average student in the public schools. Even the best of the experimental programs weren't showing much effect once the child got to be eight or nine years of age. This reinforced our notion that speaking educationally, three years was an advanced age in the lifetime of a new person. Therefore, both our own research and the results of the large scale educational experiments in the late 1960's and early 1970's forced us to take a closer look at the first few years of life.

For decades, it had been reasonably well-established within the field of developmental psychology that during the first few years of life, processes of vital lifelong importance were undergoing very special development. The most conspicuous of these was the development of language, three-quarters of which should be fully developed by the third birthday (language development very often does not progress as well as it could). The second major, and equally vulnerable, developmental process was that of early socialization. The maternal deprivation studies of the 1940's and 1950's had clearly established the time period of the first few years of life as fundamental for the construction of basic emotional security and interpersonal style. Finally, the brilliant work of Piaget performed in the 1920's and 1930's, combined with the work of students of the measurement of intelligence, indicated most clearly that by three years of age, children very often had fallen so far behind in the development of intelligence that they were not at all likely to ever fully recover lost ground.

The addition of these fundamental findings to our conclusions about our own research and that of the Head Start efforts made for a most powerful case, in our minds, which can be stated quite concisely. <u>The first educational goal for any national system should be to help each child become the best possible all-around three-year-old person.</u>

Our work on the Harvard Preschool Project, which took place in the thirteen years between 1965 and 1978, combined with our preceding work on the first six months of life and the results of quite a number of other outstanding research studies done in several countries, culminated in a wonderful success in the state of Missouri. Between 1981 and 1985, working with the personnel of the State Department of Education -- most conspicuously Commissioner Arthur Mallory and Mrs. Mildred Winter -- and the extraordinary support of Mrs. Jane Paine of the Danforth Foundation of St. Louis, we put our best research ideas into practice with some 320 Missouri families of all kinds. The project, known as "New Parents as Teachers," was a parent education and support program which began just before the first child was born. It featured a good deal of training, on the average of once a month until the child turned three years of age. There were some 40 private contacts in the home and approximately 20 group get-togethers at a center over the better than three years of our participation. The project also featured comprehensive educational monitoring of development such that if anything were to go wrong developmentally with any of the children, their parents would learn about it rather quickly and would get any needed help to deal with it.

An evaluation was performed as the children turned three years of age by an independent research team who knew nothing of which children were in the project and which were not. The results were considerably better than we had hoped. Project children ranked in the 75th percentile in mental processing and the 85th percentile in school-related achievement. They also scored significantly higher on all measures of intelligence achievement, auditory comprehension, verbal ability, and language ability than comparison children. They looked better socially, but our measures simply are too weak for us to make strong claims for them in this area.

We publicized these results extensively on the assumption that envy was more likely to produce the spread of these programs than any other factor. The State Department of Education personnel have received well over 6,000 inquiries from all over the world concerning the project. Furthermore, the state legislature passed a remarkable new law in June of 1985, making it mandatory that all 546 school

205

districts across the state offer this kind of training to everyone with one or more children under three years of age. <u>This law is the first of its kind in the world</u>.

Unfortunately, the actions of the state educational system in the months that followed were, in my judgment, quite ill-advised. The pilot projects, of which there were four, in general, were well done. The personnel were carefully selected and trained over an extensive period of time, and they also were rather well-supervised for four years. While the budgets were never overly generous, they were at least somewhat realistic. Undoubtedly, one of the key factors in the success of the pilot projects was that we only worked with first-time expectant adults (in our experience, by far the most highly motivated and easy to work with).

Having insisted that everybody have access to such programs, the state subsequently went on to create types of programs very different from those in the pilot stages. Instead of an $800 per family budget, the state allocated $165 per child and hoped that the various school districts would supplement those funds. They were, of course, well aware that most of them would not supplement them at all. It would be a most unusual school district that came near matching the budget of the pilot projects. There was no money whatsoever allocated for training, and at best, project personnel could look forward to perhaps ten full-time days of training, in contrast to the 49 or so days given under my direct supervision during the pilot stages.

Finally, the educational task was much more difficult in the statewide program than in the pilot projects. In the statewide program, many of the sites were obliged to serve populations that were predominantly high risk, most sites were involved with families who were entering the program with two children, etc. Put simply, the state attempted a much more difficult job with about one-fifth of the resources needed.

Nevertheless, the results of the pilot projects still stand. During those early stages, wonderful curriculum materials were created, along with sensible procedures, making it possible for anyone with the proper resources to replicate the truly high quality work of the pilot stages. In several locations across this country, there is developmental work oriented toward this type of replication. Whether or not they will be successful remains to be seen.

While I am naturally disappointed by the peculiar aftermath of the pilot projects in Missouri, I am not at all discouraged. Indeed, I am optimistic for the long run. I am also absolutely delighted to have the research in which I have been engaged for almost 30 years impressively confirmed -- at least in part -- by the independently evaluated Missouri "New Parents as Teachers" project. I remain totally convinced that no work is more important nor fundamental for the best long-term outcome for the quality of future people than to help their parents provide sensible, soundly based educational experiences in the period between birth and the third birthday. The Missouri project shows that to a good degree we know how to do this job. Parents and professionals in early childhood education value the goal of a delightful, capable three-year-old in such fashion and in such depth that I am quite confident that, as the years go by, these ideas will become more firmly rooted and more widely implemented.

References

LaCrosse, E. R., White, B. L., Lee, P. C., Litman, F., Ogilvie, D. M., & Stodolsky, S. The First Six Years of Life: A Report on Current Research and Educational Practice. Genetic Psychology Monographs, 1970, 82, 161-266.

Maslow, A. H. Motivation and Personality (2nd Edition). New York: Harper & Row, 1970.

White, B. L. Human Infants: Experience and Psycohological Development. Englewood Cliffs, N. J.:Prentice-Hall, 1971.

White, B. L. The First Three Years of Life. Englewood Cliffs, N. J.: Prentice-Hall, 1975; Revised Edition, 1985.

White, B. L. Educating the Infant and Toddler. Lexington, Mass.: D. C. Heath & Company, 1988.

White, B. L., Kaban, B., & Attanucci, J. The Origins of Human Competence: The Final Report of the Harvard Preschool Project. Lexington, Mass.: Lexington Books, 1979.

PUBLICATION BIBLIOGRAPHY

Sensory deprivation and visual speed: an analysis. With R. Held. Science, 1959, 130, 860-861.

Observations on the development of visually-directed reaching. With P. Castle and R. Held. Child Development, 1964, 35, 349-364.

Visual exploratory behavior following postnatal handling of human infants. With P. Castle. Percept. Mot. Skills, 1964, 18, 497-502.

Visual accommodation in human infants. With H. Haynes and R. Held. Science, 1965, 148, 528-530.

Visual pursuit and attention in young infants. With P. Wolff. J. Am. Acad. Child Psychiat., 1965, 4, 473-484.

Plasticity of sensorimotor development in the human infant. With R. Held. In The Causes of Behavior: Readings in Child Development and Educational Psychology, Ed. by Judy F. Rosenblith and Wesley Allinsmith, Boston: Allyn & Bacon, Inc., 2nd ed., 1966.

Second order problems in studies of perceptual development. In the Proceedings of a Conference sponsored by the Institute for Juvenile Research, Illinois State Department of Mental Health and National Institute of Child Health and Human Development - National Institute of Health, 1966, 523.

Informal education during the first months of life. In Hess, R. D., & R. M. Bear (Eds.), The Challenge of Early Education: Reports of Theory, Research, and Action. Chicago, Ill.: Aldine Press, 1967.

An experimental approach to the effects of experience on early human behavior. In Hill, J. P. (Eds.), Minnesota Symposium on Child Psychology, Minneapolis, MN: Univ. of Minnesota Press, 1967, 1, 201-225.

The role of experience in the behavioral development of human infants: current status and recommendations, 1967 (unpublished).

Pre-School Education - a plea for common sense. Presented at the annual meeting of the National Association of Independent Schools, New York, March 4, 1967 (unpublished).

A drawing board approach to early education. In Pintus, J. A. (Ed.), Climate for Learning. The Teacher as a Person, Report of the Thirty-Second Educational Conference, Sponsored by the Educational Bureau, 1967. Danville, Ill.: The Interstate Printers Publishers, Inc., 1968.

An apparatus for eliciting and recording the eyeblink, with Kitty Riley Clark. In Ammons, Caroll H. (Ed.), Psychological Reports - Perceptual and Motor Skills, 1968, 27, 959-964.

The initial coordination of sensorimotor schemas in human infants -- Piaget's ideas and the role of experience. In Flavell, J. H. & D. Elkind (Eds.), Studies in Cognitive Development: Essays in Honor of Jean Piaget. New York, New York: Oxford University Press, 1969, 237-256.

Child Development Research: An edifice without a foundation. In Sigel, Irving (Ed.), Merrill-Palmer Quarterly, Detroit, Michigan: The Merrill-Palmer Institute, Jan. 1969, 15, 47-78.

The Harvard Preschool Project: An etho-ecological study of the development of competence. With LaCrosse, E. R., P. C. Lee, Frances Litman, D. M. Ogilvie, Symposium presented at the Society for Research in Child Development, Santa Monica, CA, March 26-29, 1969, (unpublished).

The first six years of life: a report on current research and educational practice, with LaCrosse, E. R., P. C. Lee, Frances Litman, D. M. Ogilvie, Susan S. Stodolsky, Gen. Psychol. Monogr., 1970, 82, 161-266.

Manual for Quantitative Analysis of Tasks of One- to Six-Year-Old Children. With Barbara Kaban, Harvard Preschool Project, April, 1971.

Human Infants: Experience and Psychological Development. Englewood Cliffs, New Jersey: Prentice-Hall, Inc., 1971.

Experience and the development of motor mechanisms in infancy. In Connoly, K. (Eds.), Mechanisms of Motor Skills Development, London, England: Academic Press, 1971, 95-136.

An analysis of excellent early educational practices: preliminary report. In Effrat, Andrew (Ed.), INTERCHANGE, Toronto, Canada: The Ontario Institute for Studies in Education, 1971, 2, No. 2.

High Payoff Likely on Money Invested in Early Childhood Education. Editorials: When Should Schooling Begin? Phi Delta Kappan, June, 1972, LII, No. 10, 610-614.

Childrearing practices and the development of competence. With Barbara Kaban, Janice Marmor, and Bernice Shapiro. The Harvard Preschool Project Final Report, Grant No. CG-9909, Office of Economic Opportunity - Head Start Division, and the Carnegie Corporation of New York, Sept. 1972.

Fundamental early environmental influences on the development of competence. In Meyer, Merle E. (Ed.), Third Symposium on Learning: Cognitive Learning, Western Washington State College, 1972, 79-104.

Experience and Environment: Major Influences on the Development of the Young Child, Volume I. With Jean Watts, et al. Englewood Cliffs, N. J.: Prentice-Hall, Inc., 1973.

Early detection of educational handicaps. In de la Cruz, F. F., Fox, B. H., & Roberts, R. H., Minimal Brain Dysfunction, Annals of the New York Academy of Science, New York Academy of Science, ANYAA9, 205 (1973), 109-123.

Play activities and the development of competence during the first years of life. This paper was presented at the Georgia Symposium on Play and Exploratory Behavior held at the Georgia State University, Atlanta, GA on Jan. 25, 1973.

Preschool: has it worked? In Chaffee, J. (Ed.), COMPACT Magazine, Denver, CO: The bimonthly magazine of the Education Commission of the States, July/August, 1973.

A Training Program to Assist People in Educating Infants, with Barbara Kaban, Bernice Shapiro and Elizabeth Constable. Harvard Preschool Project, March, 1974 (mimeo).

Adult Assessment Scales and Manual for Adult Assessment Scales, with Barbara Kaban, Bernice Shapiro, Elizabeth Constable and Jane Attanucci. Harvard Preschool Project, March, 1974 (mimeo).

Reassessing our Educational Priorities. An edited transcript of an oral presentation to the Education Commission of the States Early Childhood Education Symposium held in Boston, Mass., August 3-4, 1974, and published in COMPACT Magazine, the bimonthly magazine of Education Commission of the States, 1975.

Childrearing Practices and the Development of Competence. With Barbara Kaban, Bernice Shapiro, Elizabeth Constable, Jane Attanucci and Mary Comita. The Harvard Preschool Project Final Report, Grant No. OCD-CB-193, U. S. Office of Child Development, December, 1974.

What we know about infants and what we need to know. Paper prepared for the Texas Conference on Infancy at the Joe C. Thompson Conference Center, Austin, Texas, June 22-24, 1975. (mimeo)

Critical influences in the origins of competence. Paper presented at the Merrill-Palmer Institute Conference on Research and Teaching of Infant Development, Feb. 6-8, 1974, and published in the Merrill-Palmer Quarterly, Vol. 21, No. 4, 1975.

The First Three Years of Life. Englewood Cliffs, N. J.: Prentice-Hall, Inc. (October, 1975).

Competence and Experience. With B. Kaban, B. Shapiro and J. Attanucci. In: Uzgiris I. C. & Weizmann, F. (Eds.), The Structuring of Experience, Plenum Press, 1977.

The Family: The Major Influence on the Development of Competence. An edited transcript of an oral presentation at a conference sponsored by the Edward A. Uhrig Foundation in honor of the outstanding contribution of Dr. A. B. Schwartz to Pediatrics and the Milwaukee Community, held in Milwaukee, Wisconsin, May 20, 1976.

Guidelines for Parent Education, 1977. Paper prepared for the Planning Education Conference, Flint, Michigan, September 29, 1977.

Early Stimulation and Behavioral Development. In: Oliverio, A. (Ed.), Genetics, Environment and Intelligence, Elsenier/North Holland Biomedical Press, (1977).

Center for Parent Education Newsletter - Editor. Bi-monthly publication of the Center for Parent Education, Newton, Mass, 1978 - present.

Experience and Environment: Major Influences on the Development of the Young Child, Volume II, with Barbara Kaban, Jane Attanucci, and Bernice Shapiro. Englewood Cliffs, N. J.: Prentice-Hall, Inc. (1978).

Love is Not Enough. UNESCO Courier, May, 1978.

Origins of Human Competence: The Final Report of the Harvard Preschool Project, with Barbara Kaban and Jane Attanucci. Lexington, Mass.: Lexington Books, 1979.

A Parent's Guide to the First Three Years. Englewood Cliffs, N. J.: Prentice-Hall, Inc., 1980.

The First Year of Life, with the editors of American Baby Magazine. New York, N. Y.: American Baby Books, 1981.

Should You Stay Home with Your Baby? Young Children, November, 1981.

The Origins of Competence. In: B. Shore et al, (Eds.), Face to Face with Giftedness. New York: Trillium Press, 1983.

What Is Best for the Baby ? With M. K. Meyerhoff. In: L. Dittmann (Ed.), The Infants We care For (revised edition). Washington, D. C. : NAEYC, 1984.

Competence and Giftedness. In: J. Freeman (Ed.), The Psychology of Gifted Children. Sussex, England: Wiley & Sons, 1985.

New Parents as Teachers. With M. K. Meyerhoff. In: Loving, Limiting, and Letting Go: A Guide to Parenting by the Experts of the Eighties. New York: Doubleday, 1985.

The First Three Years of Life (Revised Edition). Englewood Cliffs N. J.: Prentice-Hall, Inc., 1985.